Amber and Serena Shine were born ⌐⌐⌐ ⌐⌐⌐⌐⌐ town in the North Island of New Zealand. Together and apart, they have lived, explored and adventured abroad while juggling careers, from the New Zealand Army to Australian mining, Alaskan dog sledding and much more. Their love of the outdoors keeps them constantly adventuring – they have taken on mountains, sailed across the Pacific and survived in the wilderness, to name a few. In among their adventures, Amber, a civil engineer, is currently developing a resort at Castaways Developments, and Serena has spent the past several years building and expanding her glam camping business. They are passionate about inspiring others through their experiences, adventures and life philosophies. This is their first book.

AMBER & SERENA SHINE

THE WILD TWINS

Tales of Strength and Survival

HarperCollins*Publishers*

HarperCollins*Publishers*
Australia • Brazil • Canada • France • Germany • Holland • Hungary
India • Italy • Japan • Mexico • New Zealand • Poland • Spain • Sweden
Switzerland • United Kingdom • United States of America

First published in 2021
by HarperCollins*Publishers* (New Zealand) Limited
Unit D1, 63 Apollo Drive, Rosedale, Auckland 0632, New Zealand
harpercollins.co.nz

A catalogue record for this book is available from the National Library of New Zealand.

ISBN 978 1 7755 4176 9 (pbk)
ISBN 978 1 7754 9207 8 (ebook)

Cover design by Michelle Zaiter, HarperCollins Design Studio
Front cover photograph by Lottie Hedley
Back cover photograph by Atoni Toleafoa
Internal illustration by Serena Shine
Typeset in Bembo Std by Kirby Jones
Printed and bound in Australia by McPherson's Printing Group

Dedicated to the adventurer spirit
in all of us

Contents

Prologue

SERENA

It had to be not long after midnight, although it was hard to tell on this moonless night, with nothing but the endless African wilderness surrounding us. Carried by the wind, we could just make out the roar of a distant lion, when I heard twigs snap just outside our boma. My skin prickled in alarm as I realised a decent-sized wild animal was circling Amber and me. It seemed to be taunting us from the darkness and I prayed it was not a lion or leopard. For the first time, I felt the true fear of the hunted.

I raised my ear to the infinite darkness of the night and held my breath as I listened for the next movement, which would give away the creature's position. My heart pounded and those few moments seemed to last for an eternity. Amber and I glanced at each other in the dim firelight. We did not need to say a word. I knew with that glance we were both saying to each other, 'Be ready for the charge!'

We were in this together and we would fight off a lion together if we had to. I know how ridiculous this sounds, given we only had a machete and a bow with three arrows, but, in the heat of the moment, we had to back ourselves. There was no other option. We had to fight – there was no chance of flight against anything with four legs with our bare feet in the thorn-ridden wilderness.

I snatched up my machete and Amber grabbed an arrow in one hand and a burning piece of wood from the fire in the other. We quickly worked out how much of our wood pile we could afford to sacrifice. Our stash of firewood had to last the entire night, but it would be no use to us if we didn't survive the night ourselves. Our fire needed to be bigger to keep the predators at bay, so we threw a load of wood on it until the flames danced up as high as our waists.

When the close howl of a hyena vibrated through the air, my heart felt as though it was pounding clean out of my chest. With its powerful, wide jaw and thick neck, the hyena would have no problem ripping us to pieces.

The creature was only metres away, and our boma, which was made from spiky branches, and the fire were the only things stopping it from attacking us. My ears perked up as I heard more movement close by. Another hyena was circling in. Just how much danger was there further out in the shadows? Our imaginations started to race. Was a whole pack of hyenas waiting there for a meal of fresh meat?

We cursed at the darkness of the night; the moon wouldn't be out until the early hours of the morning, so we couldn't see anything beyond the small ring of light thrown out by our fire.

The fear, which had made the hairs on the back of my neck stand up, slowly transformed into fury as I came to terms with the danger we were in. We were sitting prey being stalked by predators.

My eyes were wide and alert, and time seemed to slow down as I calculated what we could do to fend off the growing pack. Realistically, our machete and broad-tip arrows would be no match for a single hungry hyena, let alone a whole pack of them.

On one side of our boma, there was a tree that had branches just thick enough to hold our weight; we could climb it to get off the ground. Climbing the tree would not help us escape from a lion or leopard, but if we could get high enough we might just manage to get of reach of a hyena. The tree was covered in thorns and looked impossible to climb but, given the choice of that or being attacked by a hyena, I'd take the tree every time.

We knew we had to do something to scare off the hyenas before they became brave enough to try to breach the barrier of our boma. If they did that, they'd realise we were easy pickings. Hardly able to contain our adrenaline, we readied ourselves and, on three, I smashed my machete onto our small metal pot.

The metal-on-metal sound cracked violently into the night, deafening me for a few seconds. Amber shouted aggressively and waved a branch from the fire, which sent sparks through the air. Over the commotion we were creating, we heard yelping and snarling, then the rushed movement of wild animals scurrying off.

By the light of Amber's burning branch, we could just make out the outline of two hyenas disappearing into the darkness. Their sheer size and bulk horrified us.

With our adrenaline still pumping, we looked at each other with relief. We had deterred them this time, but would they be back in a few hours? Were they only metres away, waiting for their chance to circle in again? Would our attempts at fending them off be successful in the nights to come? Given this was our first night out here, what else would we be faced with in order to survive?

Introduction

AMBER AND SERENA

This book shares with you some of the adventures we've had all over the world. From running the world's highest marathon at Mount Everest base camp to dog sledding in Michigan, from climbing New Zealand's highest mountain to surviving in the South African wilderness, we share with you a bunch of our wild, crazy escapades as well as some of the trials and tribulations we've experienced along the way.

We also share some of the valuable lessons we've learnt, and our take on what we believe life is all about and how to live it to its fullest. We think we've figured out a thing or two about how to enjoy a fulfilling life and we want to pass this on to others.

Through our adventures and wild experiences, we'd love to inspire others to seek out adventure, to motivate people to get out into the outdoors, in the technology-free fresh air, and to spend more time in nature. One of our essential messages is that it's not always easy, so don't give up, and always remember that it is often the journey itself that makes the destination worthwhile. It's all about doing more of what you enjoy in life, no matter what that might be. We hope that through our stories we'll inspire and empower others to live their best lives.

GROWING UP WILD

Chapter 1

Growing Up Wild

AMBER

Growing up, our parents always encouraged us to give things a whirl, to try new things, and they led the way showing us anything is possible. Living in the country meant there were lots of things to explore and plenty of adventures to be had. We grew up on a farm in rural little Aka Aka, south of Auckland, where the outdoors was our playground. We have an older sister, Chelsea, and a younger sister, Jasmine, but being twins meant we always had a best friend the same age to do everything with. Although, often, that also meant having a worst enemy to compete against, egg on and blame when we got into trouble.

When we were about five or six (or even younger if we managed to sneak away from Mum), Serena and I would go for expeditions, *walks really,* on the farm, which were huge adventures given how small we were. We never knew what we would find on those walks – each time something different would keep us entertained, like a hole in the ground that *could* have any creature imaginable living in it (but usually just a rabbit), a new tree to climb, a hut to build or a bird's nest to be investigated. We always seemed to go home covered in mud, scratches and grazes.

When we were just able to walk, we would venture out with Mum at night when it was raining and go snail hunting in the vegetable garden, and Dad would take us rabbit and possum shooting. From a really young age, Mum or Dad would take all four of us girls out on the farm and we'd build shelters in the bush. Then when we were a little older and after learning the ropes, Serena and I would venture out on the farm and have little adventures set for us by Mum and Dad – things like building double-storey batten huts to eat our lunch in, going into the bush to see if we could make shelters good enough to sleep in or making traps. We also loved to make rafts on which we attempted to get across the pond in front of the house, and we enjoyed getting into woodwork projects in Dad's shed.

By the time we were about eight years old, we would set ourselves all sorts of challenges. We would go out into the bush on a weekend, sometimes with our friends, to see if we could survive on the food we could gather and the shelter we built from branches, although most of the time we had a tent set up too. For such young kids, this was very serious stuff! We felt like we were miles from the house, all alone with no food and the responsibility for our survival in our own hands. In reality, we were really only a few paddocks away from the house and could go home whenever we wanted, which could be warranted in the event of a possum 'attack'.

On more than one occasion, we would wake in the night to hear something creeping around our tent. Every twig that broke sparked a serious conversation about what the creature might be, and we'd come up with a plan for our defence, which included having our big 'survival' knife ready. The breaking twigs were often followed by the horrible shrieking of a possum, and that was as good as a possum *attack* for us — which we laugh about now.

We would also take a 'back-up' stash of food with us in case we couldn't find anything out there. This was usually a generous supply of food like cans of spaghetti, sausages, which we could cook up on our fire, and plenty of lollies, which always got eaten. Even so, it didn't stop us thinking we were completing a serious survival challenge. Mum or Dad would usually drop in and check on us around dinner time and we thought it was great that we could put a sausage on a stick and cook it on the fire for them. They must have laughed at our 'hardcore-ness'!

Mum and Dad also taught us about money from a young age. Under their guidance, we drew up basic banking books and learnt about incomings and outgoings. If we completed our chores, each week we made $2, and then we'd try to figure out ways to earn extra money. Serena and I took to this, not only competing against each other, but also with a strong desire to make more.

From when we were about five, catching the white butterflies that ate the vegetables in Mum's garden was a big moneymaker for us. She would give us five cents per butterfly, and this was big money. We ran around in the garden for hours, bringing Mum each white butterfly so she could keep a tally. We could easily make 50 cents or even a dollar in a day, and we would be over the moon about it.

We went on to do things like set up a stall on the side of the road at Grandma and Grandad's to sell bags of the plums that we'd picked from their trees, often with our cousins. We came up with some other cunning ideas to make money. We'd call up the neighbours to ask if they needed help with any housework or gardening, and we also did some work at Nana and Pop's place.

As we got older and could operate tools like hedge cutters, we would do big days in Mum's garden. Back then, we worked harder but not smarter, so to make more money we'd work longer hours. After a while, even a 6 am start and shortening our lunch break didn't give us enough working hours in the garden, so we started getting up at 4 am and then 3 am. Eventually, it got so ridiculous that one morning we got up to go to work in the garden with head torches, before Mum had even gone to bed. We were swiftly told to get back to bed! We soon realised that those ridiculous hours were impossible to maintain. We can't help chuckling now at kind of determination.

We loved the outdoors, enjoyed anything physical and thrived on setting challenges for ourselves. As kids, we were extremely competitive, always having to get one up on each other in everything we did, large or small. As we got older, instead of competing against each other, we teamed up and competed together, taking on things like climbing mountains and skydiving. We came to realise we could take on bigger and bigger challenges together. I think that's where our whole 'give anything a crack' attitude to life came from.

We've always loved the ocean and our summer holidays were spent at the beach, where we'd swim for hours on end. Dad is a very keen fisherman, and he would spend any spare time he could on the water (and still does). Every chance we got we would go out with Dad on the boat, whether it was on the east coast during summer holidays or the west coast if the weather permitted. Mum would come out on calm days. We've taken after Mum with motion sickness; getting seasickness has always been a real battle but not enough to stop us.

From the age of about seven, we'd jump overboard to snorkel when Dad went scuba diving for crayfish. Once in the water, we'd swim along on the surface, following him around, watching him disappear under seaweed or rocks looking for crayfish. We would duck dive down from the surface to see if we could get all the way to the bottom and have competitions for who could grab some seaweed.

At the end of Dad's dive, he'd grab one of us and give us his spare regulator to breathe from and we'd cruise around the bottom, hanging onto Dad, exploring the ocean floor. This is when our love of diving started, and when we got a bit older, maybe 14 or so, we got our scuba diving certificates and our own dive gear so we could go diving with Dad.

During our school years, we didn't really enjoy classroom work, but that never stopped us from trying our hardest. We both loved sports and were open to trying new things. I reckon we must have tried most sports over the years, including soccer, netball, tennis, hockey, BMX racing, squash, motocross – you name it, we probably had a go at it. Our poor parents had four daughters each playing one or two sports at a time, which made for a lot of drop-offs and pick-ups. That's probably why they encouraged us to get our driving licences as soon as we were old enough. In fact, trying to beat Serena, I'm pretty sure I had booked myself in to sit my driver's licence test on the very first day I was legally allowed!

Growing up in the country means we've always understood the circle of life and have known where meat and the food we ate came from. I'm always surprised by how many people think meat comes from the supermarket and don't associate it with coming from an animal!

Hunting has always been a part of our lives, whether it was for pest control or for food. When we were young, Dad used to take us out to shoot rabbits and possums; then as we got older, he introduced us to hunting deer and pigs. We would take family trips to go hunting, staying with our uncle and auntie down south, where they had a block of land. Dad, our uncle and Kupu, the farm manager who has been hunting since the dawn of days, all took us out and showed us the ropes.

Over the years, we learnt a heap about hunting, including how to pack out a carcass and how to break down meat, ready for the freezer. We took pride in harvesting our own meat and living off the land as much as we could.

We were perched on a hillside overlooking a steep little valley, which disappeared down into a creek. Green bush and scrub completely covered one side of the valley, while the other side opened up into bumpy grassland before turning into rolling hills fading in the distance.

This was one of our first hunts by ourselves, and with us was Serena's partner, Atoni, who was on his first hunt. This week-long hunt was going to be a measure of the skills Serena and I had learnt over the years, and we were relying on ourselves to put meat on the table.

Before we'd headed out on the hunt, we began what has become a tradition to decide the order of who gets to shoot. The only fair way to do it: a game of paper, scissors, rock! It can be a nerve-racking little game, as the winner always gets the first shot. Unfortunately for me, I lost this time round – so the order was going to be Serena, Atoni, then me. We were going to have to see (and hopefully get) at least two deer before I got a shot at the third one. Bugger!

Serena had the first shot and took down a decent fallow buck from about 320 metres. It was a great shot and a nice-looking buck. Once we got the carcass back to our hunting quarters, we left the meat to hang for a few days before breaking it down for the freezer. The pressure was off a little now, as we knew we would have something in the freezer at the end of the trip. Like all our hunting, this was a meat hunt, so a stag with a good set of antlers would be a bonus but not necessarily the goal.

Atoni had the second shot and went for a fallow hind we'd spotted on the edge of a creek bed. He was definitely thinking about his stomach, as this is up there with the best, most tender venison you could possibly get.

After Atoni got his fallow deer on the second day, we spent the next three days hiking all over the place and covering a fair few kilometres. Most of the ground was too steep or inaccessible for our four-wheel motorbike, so we would park it each morning and set off for the day. Up hills, down hills, climbing through thick bush, bashing through low scrub, slogging through swamp, marching down riverbeds, then up more hills – we went everywhere.

By the time my shot came around, we'd been out hunting for five days. On the third day of it being my turn, morale was starting to drop while tensions were rising. After being together out in the bush for nearly a week, we were all starting to get a little bit sick of each other, and Serena and I had started bickering back and forth about which way we should go. We were on the side of a hill and were working out how to get around it so we could pop out on the other side to see if there were any deer about. The silly thing about it was that we both wanted to go the same way, just via different routes – we must have been tired.

Eventually, things got a little more heated until finally I stormed off one way and Serena stormed off the other way. Atoni was sensible enough to not be a part of any of it!

I took a route below a sharp bank on the lower half of the hill while Serena and Atoni had taken a higher route around the top of the hill, which was sparsely dotted with scrub. As I trudged around the side of the hill, I saw a small area of grass from which a slope dropped down into a steep valley about 100 metres wide.

On the far side of the valley, the land angled back up sharply to a large flat area that was smothered in long grass. Bush peeped over one side of the flat area, which dropped off down a cliff-like bank. From where I was standing, I could see trees growing on impossible angles all the way down to a creek. I could hear a waterfall and the constant chatter of birds.

Past the luscious grass on the far side of the valley, stood a deer, and not just any deer – the biggest red deer I have ever seen. At first, I thought it was a stag because of the sheer size of its bulk, but nope, it was a hind. We were after meat, so it was perfect. Game on!

In the second I spotted it, the hind spotted me too. Crap! I kicked myself that I hadn't been more stealthy. Usually, we would sneak around or over ridges, but Serena and I had been too busy arguing to be quiet.

It's amazing how quickly your heart rate can rise when adrenaline kicks in. I could hear the thud of my heartbeat in my ears. I'm sure every hunter knows that feeling of excitement and anticipation when you first spot your quarry. I steadied my breathing and all my concentration went into silently and smoothly getting into position to take a shot.

While I was trying to get into position as quickly as possible, it felt like everything was in slow motion. In reality, it took me just seconds to take in the scene, a second to drop to one knee and a second to line up my shot, then ... Boom!

Through the scope on my rifle, I saw that it was a hit straightaway. I looked up and the deer just stood there. It didn't move at all. It was almost as if it was suspended in time. It took one step … two steps … then collapsed in a heap. I'd made a clean shot. I was absolutely stoked.

Just out of curiosity, I took my rangefinder out of my pocket. I had thought the deer was about 300 metres away, and according to the rangefinder it was 312 metres – not bad!

Unfortunately, when the deer had taken its final steps, it had taken them towards the cliff and when it had collapsed, of course it had collapsed over the edge of the cliff. Unbelievable! What are the chances of that happening?

From where I stood, I heard tree branches breaking as the deer tumbled down the cliff, wiping out anything in its path, before it came to a halt. The deer was down and I was ecstatic. A smile came across my face as I fist-pumped with excitement. There's nothing quite like the feeling of a clean shot, an instant drop and knowing our freezers would be full.

Serena and Atoni had heard the shot from above as they covered the high ground. They'd waited a few minutes before coming down to my position to be sure they weren't going to spook a deer or distract me if I needed to take a second shot.

'Surely not!' Serena said. It's fair to say she didn't share my excitement after seeing it go over the cliff. With the previous arguing now forgotten, Serena had a big grin across her face, and she asked how the hell I planned to get it out of there.

'Don't worry, mate, I'll get it out,' I said.

She wasn't convinced. 'What? Back up the cliff?'

She had a point, but how was I to know it was going to fall off a cliff?

Either way, I was going to have a hell of a good go at getting it out. We never leave meat behind so, one way or another, I was determined we would get our venison out.

It must have taken us about 45 minutes to run down into the valley in front of us and then climb back up the other side to the flat grassy area where the deer had once been standing. Finally, all three of us stood there on the edge of the cliff and peered over the side.

Hmmm … there was a steep bank covered in trees and no deer in sight. We could hear the nearby waterfall louder now, and we figured the drop had to be at least 80 metres or so. The sound of the creek far below was muffled, so maybe it was further than that. The side of the cliff was covered in patches of dense bush and big sturdy trees. Surely it couldn't have bowled through the trees and made it the whole way down – could it?

Well, there was no time to waste – we had to find a way down the steep face. We walked along the lip of the ledge until we found a small, rough, scarred area less than half a metre wide that had eroded away to create what almost looked like a few steps down the five or so metres to where the dense bush began.

Without hesitation, down the ledge we went. Once we were in the trees, thick branches provided us with plenty of hand holds, but the steep angle of the descent meant it took a little negotiating to find a route.

It was incredibly slow going, proper snail's pace – well, maybe a snail on steroids! After about quarter of an hour, we had only made it down about 20 metres. We stopped and stood there – or more likely hung – for a few minutes while we pondered our next move.

As we were talking, something behind Serena's shoulder caught my eye. We had been tracking the almost undetectable scuffs marks the falling deer had left behind, but now I could see some distinctive broken branches – and then something brown caught in the trees. There she blows!

Its fall had been stopped by two solid tree trunks. Thank goodness. I knew we had a lot better chance of hauling it up the last 20 metres rather than up the entire bank and back over the ledge at the top.

We inspected the carcass, which was wedged tightly into the trees. We were all buzzing now we could see the beast I had taken down, but then I remembered the rule we have – you shoot it, you carry it out. This was going to be a true test for me. How on earth was I going to get this massive deer out?

I gave the legs a tug. It didn't move. Then I gave it a big, hearty tug, pulling with all my might. Still, it didn't move. Yep, I was in for one hell of a challenge. I decided to gut it where it hung, propped in the trees. This would lighten the load and might also mean I would actually be able to move it back up the steep bank. Boning it out was always an option as we'd be able to carry the meat out in our packs, but we decided that, if we could manage it, carrying it out whole would be easier.

I got to work slicing the belly open and removing all the insides, then lopping off the head. All this was happening as I was clinging onto the trees, trying to stay upright and prevent myself slipping down the rest of the decline. It wasn't easy! Each time I freed a part of the gut, it went tumbling down, down, down.

While I'd been hard at work, Serena and Atoni had sat there, clinging onto their trees and laughing their heads off at my struggles. Once I'd finished up, it was time to move this great mass. I gave the leg a tug again, hoping it would be light enough to move – it wasn't, damn it!

I talked Serena and Atoni into helping me out by promising I would help them with the next big one they got (yeah, right). While hanging onto our respective trees with one arm, all three of us grabbed a leg each with our free arm and hauled away. The dead weight reluctantly started to budge, and with all three of us pulling we managed to move it slightly.

On the count of three, we all gave a big heave at the same time and managed to pry it out of the clutches of the trees in which it had been wedged. It moved a good metre in the right direction. Then, bit by bit, metre by metre, struggle by struggle, we finally managed to get it up the bank, to the top of the incline, where we needed to give it one more giant shove to get it over the lip of the ledge. Serena and Atoni held it in place while I scrambled up over the ledge and could turn around to reach down to grab its front legs. With some serious huffing and puffing, me pulling the front legs up towards me, and Serena and Atoni lifting the back of the deer above their heads and pushing it up with all their might, we got it over the ledge. Finally, we could rest without worrying about slipping down the cliff. What a great feeling!

For a moment, we sat, caught our breath and laughed at our struggles. Then it was time to think about our next challenge – getting the deer back to the quad bike we had left a few kilometres back. For our next hurdle, we could either go up a very steep hill then cut across horizontally to carry on towards the bike, or we could go back the way we came, down the valley and back up the other side, which was even steeper again. Both ways were much too steep to get our four-wheeler down, and both ways looked like some seriously hard yakka. Neither was overly appealing, but we chose to go straight up the steep hill as, at least, it was a more direct route.

We used our favourite backpack technique to haul the deer out. I made incisions on the rear legs of the carcass, looped the front legs through the incisions on the rear legs, twisting them to keep them in place, turning them into two shoulder-strap loops. Then I sat down and leant back towards the carcass while I got the newly created straps over each shoulder, just like putting a backpack on. I've always found this method of retrieving a carcass by far the easiest way to carry our meat out. There's also the bonus of getting the whole deer home instead of just the meat, so nothing gets wasted. The dogs are always super happy when they get the bones.

Sitting upright, I braced myself with one hand on the ground then rolled into a kneeling position ready to heave myself up to a standing position. Despite my best effort, I barely moved. This was the first time I'd come across a deer so heavy that I couldn't stand up by myself with it on my back. I half-heartedly noted not to go for one this size again, as it felt heavier than the stags I had retrieved in the past.

With the deer strapped to my back, Serena and Atoni stood either side of me and held a shoulder each. I heaved myself to my feet while they pulled at the same time. Thankfully, I managed to stand up this time. After a few cautious steps forwards, I could feel how wobbly my knees were – the kind of wobbly that meant they might give out at any moment without any warning.

Each step was a considerable effort and with the steep terrain and uneven ground, I had to really concentrate on the placement of each foot. Sweat was pouring down my forehead in the afternoon sun as I heaved the monster up the hill. Slowly but surely, we were making our way up the hill; progress was progress.

If I tripped or fell while carrying this kind of weight over such steep ground, there would be no stopping me. I would tumble the whole way back down the hill getting squished on each tumble.

This was not something I wanted to test out, so we came up with a safety net – Atoni. He would be close-by on the downhill side of me, ready to counteract and bump me forwards if I became unbalanced. This was a little easier for Atoni, who is a bulky guy with muscles on his muscles. He was ghosting closely behind me, so if I were to trip or if I stumbled off balance, he was ready to barge me forwards so I'd end up sitting on the uphill side of the slope instead of rolling backwards down it.

The plan worked well, but after a while, I began to tire from the effort, so Serena and Atoni helped by taking turns at carrying the deer. As I watched Serena heave it up the hill, I thought to myself how ridiculous it looked on her back, dwarfing her in comparison. How we were managing to carry it, I'm not sure. I laughed when it even made Atoni look small as he lugged it up the hill.

After few hours of burning thighs, we made it to the top of the hill (which felt more like a mountain). We could no longer see the cliff edge where we had started out far below, and we were stoked to have covered a decent amount of ground. We rested for a while, all with grins of satisfaction at having made it this far.

The quad bike was still a good few kilometres away, and we knew it would take us the rest of the afternoon to get there carrying this sort of weight, so we made a call for Serena to run back to the bike, carrying only a rifle in case she spotted another deer on the way. In the meantime, Atoni and I continued to take turns carrying the deer in an attempt to get it to a point that was more accessible for the quad bike.

After covering more ground, grunting and puffing away, I heard the faint noise of a motor. Gradually, it got louder and louder, and five minutes later, Serena came around the corner on the four-wheeler. Boy, were we happy to see her!

We tied the deer on the front of the bike then jumped on the back as Serena kicked the bike into gear. We made our way back to the hunting quarters before the evening set in. It wasn't exactly smooth sailing on the way back, as there was plenty of terrain that required us to jump off and on, and a keen eye in order to keep the bike upright.

A lot of the ground was still steep enough to be borderline for a four-wheeler to get up or down, but we made it back in one piece and still on all four wheels.

When we pulled up at the hunting quarters, Kupu came out to be greeted by our grinning faces. He could hardly believe we'd carried something of that size and joked about how half the guys he took out hunting wouldn't carry something that big out.

We hung the meat on a butcher's hook and started prepping for breaking it down into separate cuts. Before we did that though, we couldn't help our curiosity and weighed it. Gutted with no head it weighed 102 kilograms. No wonder Kupu was surprised we'd managed to carry it — that wasn't that far off Serena's and my body weights combined.

The following day, we took our time breaking down the meat and separating the cuts. We had loads of venison steaks as well as a pile of tougher meat to make into mince and sausages, and the heart and kidneys were always saved for a steak, heart and kidney pie. Kupu's dogs were pretty happy with the leftover scraps and the bones. The hide was beautiful — I took it home to have a go at curing it. Often, when hunting you come back with nothing, which really makes you appreciate the time you do well. Not only did we have plenty of meat for us and our families, but we were also thrilled with how epic the trip had been — so much so that it fuelled many of our hunts to come.

EXCELLENCE AND FIT FOR LIFE

We love the quote, 'We are what we repeatedly do. Excellence, therefore, is not an act but a habit.' We believe that if you are going to do something, you might as well do it to the best of your abilities. If you take on everything in this way, it soon becomes an effortless habit.

It takes a similar amount of energy to do something poorly as it does to do the same task to a high level, so you might as well do everything to the best of your abilities. It's amazing what you discover you can do when you put in the effort.

This can be carried through to many aspects of life; one of the things we have consistently worked on turning into an effortless habit is maintaining our health and wellbeing. After all, none of the material things really matter if you don't have your health.

Given we like being able to take off on adventures at a moment's notice, a big part of health and wellbeing for us is making sure we're fit for life. This means we consistently maintain a level of fitness that works for our lifestyle and means we are always in shape for anything we want to do. It also means we don't need a huge amount of time to train from square one every time we decide to take on a new adventure, as we are always ready. Being fit and healthy, in general, also has the benefit of being less at risk of getting injured because you are always conditioned for the task you take on.

Being fit for life also makes day-to-day life more enjoyable. It means that the daily things you do are easier, and you don't risk hurting yourself when you do the off-one things like lifting heavy boxes into the car or spending a whole day in the garden. It also makes a huge difference when things happen that we can't prepare for like injuries or other life setbacks.

During our school years, we played a lot of sports and, after that, we got into CrossFit. We found that CrossFit suited our lifestyle as it can be both competitive and social. It prepares us for adventures by working on both strength and cardio at the same time, giving us the best of both worlds.

While CrossFit works for us, anything that helps you to retain a good level of fitness is great, whether it be cycling, yoga or regular walking. It's all about finding what works for you and the lifestyle you want to lead.

Another important part of being fit for life is nutrition. We believe in fuelling your body with the good stuff (the majority of the time, anyway). After all, you wouldn't put a two-stroke in a Ferrari, so don't settle when it comes to your body.

Foodwise, we keep it simple by not having too much of any one thing, eating whole and natural foods whenever possible and only having treats every now and then.

Nutrition and fitness can impact both our physical and mental health, so we consistently work on them to ensure we are able to maintain our lifestyles and retain our quality of life.

INTO THE WORLD AND EXPLORING

Chapter 2

Into the World and Exploring

New Zealand and Australia

AMBER

After we left school, Serena and I tried a few different things before settling into our careers. The different fields we worked in allowed us to get well-rounded life experience and we were able to figure out what we enjoyed doing. We started discovering what life was about before making big commitments to our particular career paths. When we left college, neither of us had any idea what we wanted to do in life. We did well in all our school subjects, so this didn't narrow things down for us. We both enjoyed sports and the outdoors, but had no idea how to relate that to the real world.

The thought of going to university to study something we weren't sure if we liked seemed too daunting. We were both ambitious and were in a hurry to get somewhere – but we had no idea where that was. There was nothing that we could positively say, 'Yep, I want to do that.' We went to all sorts of careers days, work experience trips and university open days, but there was just nothing that stuck.

During our last year at school, we decided to have a go at the two-week officer selection course for the New Zealand Army. With its combination of physical work, use of weapons and being paid to keep fit, the army really appealed to us.

Curiously, officer selection was the first time we realised just how 'twinsie' we were. During the two weeks of selection testing, we were separated into different groups and hardly saw each other. During selection, we did numerous tests and tasks and were put into a heap of tricky situations while psychologists watched our reactions and officers critiqued the solutions we came up with.

We were later told they had kept a close eye on us because we reacted in exactly the same ways and offered the exact same solutions in multiple situations. Having scrutinised our every move, the mediators eventually concluded that it had been impossible for us to have communicated with each other and that as well as looking the same, our brains worked the same way too. We were as surprised as they were!

We were among the few people who passed selection, but we were only 17 years old and needed to be at least 18 to start officer training, so we decided to spend a year getting some experience as soldiers before switching over to train as officers.

Independently, we both decided to join as combat engineers. It was the most appealing corps as we'd learn a variety of engineering skills while still being in the thick of the combat side of things.

After our officer testing, the army decided we were too similar to go into the same corps, so one of us would have to decide on something else. We were beside ourselves. We had no need or want to stick together – we never have in our careers. It just happens that a lot of the time we choose the same things independent of one another simply because we are interested in the same things.

Can you imagine finally deciding what you want to do, getting all excited about it, then being told, 'No, your sibling does that, and you can't both do it'?

The fight over who got to be a combat field engineer could only be settled in one way, the only fair way we ever settle anything: a game of paper, scissors, rock. We've always found this to be a great way to settle things as it's a game that fate decides. There is no way to cheat at paper, scissors, rock and no way anyone can have an advantage. It's as fair as fair can be. So, after an extremely nerve-wracking game, Serena won. Bummer!

So, straight out of school, we joined the New Zealand Army. Serena joined as a combat field engineer and I joined as a gunner in the Royal New Zealand Artillery. While I was gutted not to be a field engineer, training to be a gunner was a great old time with a lot of adventure, running around, shooting things and blowing things up.

We were both based in Waiouru, but as we were in different basic training intakes and different corps, it was rare for us to see each other. Nonetheless, that year was marvellous as we learnt a lot and got paid to keep fit. Brilliant!

Before the year was up, an opportunity had popped up for me that left me with a decision to make. I knew I could switch over to train as an officer at the end of the year; however, I came out of basic training with the award for top solider out of 122 males and 22 females. As a result of this award, I was offered a choice, which isn't common in the army; I could either switch over to officer training, as I had initially planned, or I could be deployed to East Timor and have the opportunity to serve overseas.

It was a no-brainer for me. Officer training would still be there the following year, but a lot of soldiers serve for years without getting a deployment opportunity. I spent the next six months or so serving in East Timor, which was one hell of an experience, for both highs and lows came with it.

Serena was having blast as a combat field engineer, so she stuck with it for the next year, learning a variety of skills like clearing minefields, building improvised explosive devices, and setting booby traps and clearing them effectively. She also did tons of bridge building and would go on all sorts of training missions that involved things like stealthily advancing up rivers in unmarked boats in the middle of the night with night-vision goggles, dropping off stores along the way.

When I returned from serving overseas, we'd been in the army for nearly two years and we were starting to think about what else was out there. Eventually, Serena and I were finally able to have a good catch up, which is when we realised we'd been having the exact same thoughts – we'd both figured out we weren't cut out for being told what to do all the time.

Our initial excitement at learning to use weapons and blowing things up had worn off and the old 'hurry up and wait' attitude, which was common in the army, was getting harder and harder to tolerate. We decided enough was enough and it was time to think about doing something new.

We were no closer to figuring out what we wanted to do in life, so we decided to chase the money and headed across the ditch to make some Aussie coin and get into the booming mining industry. In hindsight, this worked out to be a rather good move, as making reasonable money meant we had the means to fund some epic adventures, which was a priority for us.

At the time, heading to another country, with not a lot to our names, no jobs and knowing no one, was a big move for us. We realised that although we had gained some great life experiences in the army, it didn't really give us any sort of qualifications for the outside world. This is one of the reasons a lot of ex-military personnel can have a bit of a rough ride transitioning back into civilian life.

Leaving the army wasn't made any easier by my superiors at the time. My commanding officer told me I'd regret it and I'd never get another job as good as this one. My sergeant also told me I would never amount to anything if I was silly enough to leave. Serena had a similar experience and was told she was dreaming if she thought she would get a job in the mines.

Before we left for Perth, numerous people cautioned us that we'd struggle to get jobs in the mines unless we knew someone and had contacts. In our usual fashion, we were determined to make it happen in any case and headed to Australia with a 'she'll be right' attitude.

Well, apparently, you did have to know someone, and it seemed everyone knew someone in the mines ... apart from us. While relentlessly chasing jobs in the mines, we spent months picking up any temporary work we could get. We worked in factories, did landscaping and then started driving big trucks to drop off loads of construction goods to the high-rise buildings going up all over the central city.

Eventually, our persistence and willingness to take a punt at anything paid off and we made it into the mines. We started out as dumptruck drivers in an underground gold mine in Kambalda, about 60 kilometres from Kalgoorlie in Western Australia.

We spent a couple of years working underground in the gold mine, and during that time we worked our way up through the different levels as we got more experience. We went from working as service crew (fixing anything in the mine), to being leading hands with a couple of guys on a crew under us and then on to shot firing (working with explosives, blowing up tunnel faces). Just as we had in the army, we worked at the same place, in similar roles independent of each other. Again, we barely saw one another as we worked fly-in fly-out from Perth on opposite shifts.

Being in a 6-kilometre tunnel underground was quite eerie, and we could easily go a whole two-week shift of

12-hour days without seeing daylight. The first week of shift was nightshift, so we spent the whole night working underground and then the whole day sleeping. For the second week, we would transition to dayshift where we still spent the whole 12-hour day underground in a dark hole and it would be almost dark by the time we came back up to the surface.

In the meantime, we took on anything else we could learn, and part of this was becoming mine rescue volunteers. This was something we both really enjoyed and, having had enough of being underground, we both transitioned into working in emergency rescue full time. For the next few years, we worked in open pit mines instead of underground, which was a welcome change.

As emergency services officers, we did everything rescue-related in the mines and the surrounding area, including fire-fighting, rope rescue, underground rescue, vehicle extraction and running the medical centre, which involved a lot of medical and first responder work as well. Many of the skills we learnt in the mines have come in handy during our adventures.

We stayed in the mines almost twice as long as we'd originally planned. It felt like we just blinked and our two years became four years. During our time off, we had plenty of adventures together. We got our solo skydiving licences and would spend our weeks off jumping out of planes over Perth or exploring the outback. We would go rock climbing on old quarry faces, camping in the middle of nowhere or diving up north.

Over the years, the list of things Serena and I wanted to do had got bigger and bigger, so once we were out in the world, there was no stopping us. Eventually, those adventures became more and more extreme. Pretty soon, we were mountaineering, ice climbing, skydiving, rock climbing and travelling to all sorts of weird and wonderful places to explore.

Travelling is great for getting an insight into different cultures and a well-rounded perspective about the world. Experiencing the different ways people live in different environments certainly keeps you grounded and gives you a humble outlook on life.

The coin in the mines was great and the adventures it funded during our weeks off were even greater, but we wanted to build something of our own. During our time in the mines, we'd both managed to figure out the career path we wanted to head towards. I had pondered civil engineering when leaving school but didn't know enough about it at the time. Our father is a civil engineer by trade, so I guess it kind of came naturally to me. I had been able to spend a bit of time with engineers during my years in the mines and previous to that, and I decided that civil engineering was the right direction for me. I did a university degree, studying full time through correspondence, which I fitted around my work in the mines.

Studying through correspondence, working through the textbooks myself and watching the lectures online meant I spent many late nights and early mornings studying, but I could work it in around my job then fly to Queensland to meet the on-campus students and sit the exams.

I couldn't handle the thought of studying on campus when I knew I could achieve the same thing while working it around my life. Other students used to say, 'It's great, you get two free periods a day, so you only have to do four or five classes in a day.' That didn't sound great to me, as I was not keen on sitting on campus having free periods while waiting for afternoon classes. I wanted to be out in the world while getting my degree as fast as I could.

Correspondence isn't for everyone, but it was the perfect solution for me. Working full time funded my study, so I didn't have to take out a student loan. I must admit it did mean I had no life for quite a while, as all I did was work or study, so it certainly wouldn't be for everyone.

I would get up at 3 or 4 am to put in a few hours of study before my shift at the mine started. On my week off back in Perth, while everyone was out having fun, I would be studying – but you gotta do what you gotta do.

While I was studying and working, Serena and I discussed several ideas for starting our own business in Perth. We would put a tonne of time and work into our due diligence making sure an idea was thoroughly researched and planned before taking the plunge. Of these, we were extremely close to pulling the trigger on two, and for one of them Serena worked part time and became qualified in the field on her week off from the mines, so we had hands-on experience before we started out our own, but life was to have other ideas.

When dealt an unexpected hand in life, which you'll read about in Chapter 5, Serena moved back to New Zealand for the long road of recovery. She went in with our father on a business idea and started up her own successful luxury glamping business called Glam Camping at Castaways, near where we grew up. Soon she expanded it to a glamping village, hosting all sorts of events.

After graduating as a civil engineer, I'd had enough of studying at all sorts of crazy hours while simultaneously working 12-hour shifts in the mines. I took a few years off for travel before coming home to New Zealand to work as a civil engineer. I went on to join the family development project, and now I run Castaways Developments, an ongoing project expanding Castaways Resort.

Looking back at our first years of working experience, trying so many different things shaped us to become all-rounders who now run our own businesses. The life experience we gained in the process was priceless. These jobs took us all around the world on all sorts of adventures that, when we started out, we could never have imagined. The chapters that follow are just a handful of our favourites.

DECIDING WHAT YOU WANT TO DO IN LIFE

A piece of advice I would give to anyone trying to figure out which path to take is to get out into the world and try a few different things before deciding on what you want to do in life. There are so many things out there to experience, and the more we try things, the more we expand our horizons, discover what we enjoy and find out what we are good at.

Getting out of college and into the real world can be daunting for some people, especially if they are unsure of which career path or direction to take. Some people know exactly what they want to do, which is great, and they will get straight into their desired career or studying for it.

People who don't know what they want to do are often left wondering how they are supposed to choose what they want to do in life without getting out into the world yet. Rather than taking a stab in the dark and diving headfirst into a big commitment if you're unsure, you might be better off going out into the world, trying a few different things and figuring out what you like doing, what you don't like doing and what your strengths are.

There is no rush for you to start a career, especially as you may end up doing it for the rest of your life. With this in mind, getting work and/or world experience before committing a huge amount of your time, effort or money to your chosen career can go a long way.

Everyone has different needs, wants and priorities, and there are no rules for anything, no set lengths of time to do things and no right or wrong paths – so don't be afraid to go against the grain!

MOUNT EVEREST BASE CAMP

Chapter 3

Mount Everest Base Camp

Nepal

AMBER

We woke early, to the hum of the storm shaking the walls of our lodgings. I crawled out of my sleeping bag and jumped off the hard mattress, then riffled through my pack for some warmer gear to throw on. Serena had spent most of the night lying awake, shivering, and I hadn't been much better off. Despite our lack of sleep, we both felt energised and excited as we pulled on our boots, readying ourselves for the day's climb. My breath misted, forming a cloud in front of me on every exhale, and my nose was pink from the cold. The incoming storm had brought in a fresh blanket of snow, now covering the trail, making it difficult to see.

After breakfast, we stood there, heavy packs on our backs and ready to set off for the day. We were looking out at the brutal weather conditions, nervous but invigorated by what the day might bring us. The oxygen felt odd in my lungs, like I couldn't quite take a big enough breath to feel comfortable, or maybe it was that my lungs couldn't expand to let enough oxygen in. It was the altitude for sure, I knew that much.

We were standing over 5000 metres above sea level, on our way to base camp on the world's highest mountain: Mount Everest. We had been hiking for the last three days and we were now only two days, perhaps, from base camp. It was May 2014, and we were just discovering our love of the mountains. We had both read a book about Mount Everest, which had excited us, and were eager to check it out for ourselves.

Climbing the mountain one day had come up in our conversations every now and then, so this hike up to base camp was a little bit of a reccy for us to check out the mountain and find out what it was all about.

The view that morning did not disappoint – through the stormy white haze, we could just make out the mountains towering above us. Serena and I agreed to push on through the storm, our theory being that we didn't want to wait until the weather got so bad that we could no longer move up the mountain. We wanted to gun it and get as high as we could before being stuck in one spot for what could be a few days. It was an understatement calling the weather a tad miserable, but we were still low enough on the mountain that it wasn't a safety concern ... yet. If we left now, there was a good chance of making it to the next village or even to base camp before the storm set in fully. We talked to our guide, a local Nepalese chap, and he agreed with our plan to keep moving.

We set off into the howling wind and within the first few steps a sharp gust of wind whipped my hood off. I quickly grabbed at it, pulling the drawstrings tight before the sideways-blowing snow could make it to my ears. It was exhilarating at first, the novelty of the storm adding to the adventure. We chuckled at each other as we battled our way upwards, fresh and full of energy. With the snow in our faces and the wind taking the breath out of our mouths, we fought to take each step against the force of the wind in order to push higher and higher up the mountain.

Our guide was very familiar with the route, so he was able to break a trail through the heavy snow without hesitation, even though the visibility was only 20 metres at best. The trail swirled up the mountain. It was a very narrow path, barely a metre wide, cut horizontally into the steep slope. There was a steep bank on one side and a straight drop off on the other. As the snow collected on the lip of the drop-off, it created the effect of a false ledge, which would have been very easy to step on. Anyone who did that would have ended up hurtling down the cliffside, which is not something we wanted to test out. We watched our guide closely. He never put a foot wrong, which gave us confidence in following the trail he was cutting. This clearly wasn't his first rodeo.

A few hours in, the novelty and excitement had worn off. We were huffing and puffing and our legs were burning under the weight of our packs, which were now clogged with snow. They seemed to be growing in weight every minute as the melting snow made them progressively wetter.

The corner of my eyes stung as the wind whipped icy droplets into my face, and the roar of the weather meant I couldn't hear anything apart from my own puffing. I tried to ignore how numb my fingers were inside my gloves as I brushed snow off my shoulders. I could feel the moisture creep in as the snow melting on my shoulders was starting to soak through my clothes.

Serena was behind me and, when I looked back, I saw that she was totally white with snow as the flakes landed on her shoulders. I yelled back to her to check she was OK but couldn't make out her reply. With a hearty smile, she shot back a thumbs up, and we carried on upwards.

As we hiked on, I overheated with the effort of climbing and all my layers of clothing became damp with sweat. If we stopped at all, even for a second, the sweat instantly turned ice cold as the wind ripped past us. We had to keep moving through our growing exhaustion so as not to freeze from our own cooling sweat.

At one point, we came around a corner and noticed a small group of locals, who had climbed about 50 metres down a cliff. They were all huddled around something. As we watched, one of them climbed back up to the trail. He was covered in blood and had a large butcher's knife in his hand. Holy heck!

Serena and I looked at each other, puzzled. The guide explained that a yak, a heavily built type of cattle used to cart stores up the mountain, had fallen off the cliff in the rough weather and died. At this sort of altitude, meat was hard to come by and the villagers used everything. Nothing went to waste.

We carried on and pushed hard through the weather and, by lunchtime, we had made it to a small village consisting of only a few local teahouses offering food, drink and a place to stay. Soaked through from both our own sweat and the snow, we welcomed the chance to rest under some shelter and warm up over lunch.

We had hiked up and out of the worst of the snow storm, so we wondered whether we should keep pushing up instead of staying here the night. It looked like the weather was better higher up and we could see it was really settling in below where we had just come from. The guide confirmed our suspicions and recommended we keep going up as quickly as possible while we still could. If the horrendous weather below us changed direction and started moving up, it was possible we could get stranded here for a few days, which would mean we'd miss out on getting to base camp. We agreed this was a good plan and braced ourselves in anticipation of getting back out into the weather.

As we scoffed down our crackers and salami and sipped hot tea, we watched as another group began to argue with their guide. The group was panicking about the bad weather coming in and wanted to descend immediately. They didn't care about getting to base camp anymore – they just wanted to get the hell out. I am not sure they had thought through their argument – it seemed a little odd to descend directly into what we could now see was the eye of the storm, which looked even worse than what we had just hiked through.

Their guide was attempting to explain to them how tough it would be heading down into the weather and that their best option would be to stay put were they were warm and comfortable while it blew over. The group had clearly made up their minds and wouldn't listen to any advice.

On top of this, they were demanding that their guide arrange for donkeys or horses to take them back down. You have got to be joking. They wanted to ride a donkey – in this weather! I couldn't think of anything worse, especially given what we'd just seen with the yak down the cliff. I would never trust a donkey to get me down; it wasn't a straightforward trail and all it would take was one false step to fall off a cliff.

Eventually, their guide gave up trying to advise them and agreed to their demands. We watched on with interest as they hopped onto their donkeys and set off towards the heart of the blizzard. It was a sorry sight, the tiny horses and donkeys struggling under the weight of the large group. It was a disaster waiting to happen.

Thankfully, that disaster didn't occur, because within five minutes, one of them had fallen off his donkey twice and the poor donkey was unwilling to carry his weight anymore. Standing around in the snowstorm, waiting for one of their team members to get up off the ground – twice – must have sobered the panicked group and they had turned around and were making their way back to the teahouse. I think they realised pretty quickly exactly what their guide had been trying to warn them about.

After our lunch and the free entertainment, we set off up the mountain again. We had a new surge of energy as we realised we could reach base camp before the end of the day. It was a gruelling hike through the snow, but we were on a mission.

After a few more hours of hiking towards the better weather, our eyes lit up when we started to see colourful Nepalese prayer flags strung up around the place. We were getting closer!

As we got higher than the storm, the tail end of the blizzard started to ease, and the sun was even trying to come out but not having much luck. I looked back down the mountain to where we had come from. The dark clouds that had set in below looked as angry as ever, but the storm was not moving upwards, which was welcome news for us.

With a little cheer of relief, we finally made it to the last small village where we would be staying the night – the highest teahouse on the mountain. The weather was starting to play ball now and we were seeing the first rays of sunshine trying to provide some warmth against our icy surroundings. We dropped our packs at our lodgings and continued for the last short leg to make it to base camp.

After only half an hour of eager walking, we took our first step into Mount Everest's base camp. We had made it. Little did we know this was going to be only half of our challenge …

During the hike up, I had been looking up at the world's highest mountain in awe. Now, it was so much closer, it took my breath away. From where we stood at base camp, I could see up past the ice cliffs, rocks and crevasses, right to the summit. It was a humbling sight and I took a moment to take in my surroundings.

As we stared at the summit, we were impressed by the mighty challenge it presented. The adventure to base camp had been a blast, so I made a mental note to add a summit attempt to our bucket list of things to give a crack one day.

We had expected base camp to be deserted as we were there at what was, typically, the end of the climbing season, so most summit attempts would have been completed already. Curiously, though, there were still a few tents set up. Our guide tried to explain why, but his strong accent and stretched translation meant we didn't quite grasp his explanation.

Base camp sits at 5380 metres, and we were over the moon when we saw we could go just a little higher. We climbed a short way further, then, in the beautiful sunshine that had fought its way to peek out through the clouds, we sat and took in the view. We were fascinated at picking out the route that went on, further up the mountain. We looked across to the Khumbu Icefall and admired the jagged, icy teeth of the glacier and its gaping crevasses.

As we sat and took in the view, we heard a bang, a crash then a roar bellow out across the valley as an avalanche came crashing down the icefall. It was spectacular to watch such impressive force tumble down the glacier and, thankfully, no one was anywhere near the destruction. There had been a massive avalanche on the icefall a month earlier and 16 Sherpas had been killed. This had really shaken the climbing community.

Satisfied that we had done what we had come here to do, it was time to head back down to the last teahouse we had passed in Gorak Shep, before the evening set in. The sunshine had disappeared as quickly as it had arrived, and more snow and strong winds were instantly back upon us. As the darkness crept in, we made it back down to our lodgings.

We threw off our gear and went to sit by the fire to warm up and dry out. Again, we had expected the place to be deserted, but it was packed with people of all different nationalities. We asked what everyone was up to and found out they were all up here to run the world's highest marathon. Hmmm, the world's highest marathon … interesting.

The marathon started at the Khumbu Icefall at base camp (5170 metres above sea level) then covered 42.195 kilometres down the trail we had just walked up, finishing at the village of Namche Bazar (3440 metres above sea level).

It all made sense now. This explained why there were still tents at base camp and why there was so many people in this little village. Due to the atrocious storm, many of the runners had camped here as it was slightly less exposed than base camp.

The race was called the Tenzing Hillary Everest Marathon, and it was being held on 29 May – the date Tenzing Norgay and Sir Edmund Hillary first summited the mountain in 1953. Athletes had come from all around the world to participate and there would be just as many local Nepalese runners as international ones.

Having got all the details, our minds began to tick. What was the date today? 28 May. When was this marathon? Tomorrow! Holy heck, what were the chances of arriving at base camp a day early because we'd decided to beat a blizzard, only to find out the world's highest marathon was being held here the very next day? Surely, this was meant to be.

We were exhausted after a big day of hiking, but we couldn't stop now. We had to get to the bottom of this whole marathon thing. Our day had already been eventful enough, but we weren't about to pack it in yet. We put some thought into how hazardous the trail might be, as the group had warned us it was a pretty serious event to take on. Running at altitude is completely different as there is less oxygen and the conditions would be harsh. Nah, she'll be right! We knew our limitations and how far we could push ourselves.

By this time, it was pretty late and we could hear the rough weather getting worse outside, but we'd just found out that the marathon organisers were staying in one of the huts not far from us. Our guide was shocked that we would even contemplate such a thing.

'Have you been training for a marathon?' he asked.

'No ...'

From talking to the runners, we knew that most of them had come to Nepal a few weeks early to acclimatise and get used to running at altitude and over rough terrain. On top of that, they'd also trained for months at home. OK, maybe we were a little unprepared.

Our guide then asked, 'Have you ever run a marathon before?'

'No ...'

He grinned. 'Well, you are both mad but good luck to you ... just don't die,' were his final words of wisdom to us. It was great advice: *just don't die*.

We threw on our still-damp jackets and set off into the stormy darkness to find the organisers. Knocking on the doors of the few huts in the area, we soon found them. Curious about what we wanted, they invited us into their teahouse and we were happy to get out of the torment of the weather.

Well, we had some convincing to do and we didn't have much time to do it in. We explained that we were really enthusiastic about the event and really, *really* wanted to do the marathon. They told us we couldn't as we needed to have entered months ago. Besides, we hadn't completed all the formalities like a getting a medical certificate to say we were healthy enough to run at altitude, and we hadn't paid for our entries.

We explained that we did CrossFit and had trained for the climb to base camp using altitude masks, and may have alluded to some long-distance training, so not only were we fit but we were ready for the altitude (the majority of this was true!). We also explained that we had all of our running gear ready to go as we had planned on doing a workout at base camp in any case.

After a lot of persistence and going back and forth countering their objections over the course of an hour or so, they finally ran out of reasons to say no – or maybe they were just sick of us. Either way, our persistence paid off and they finally agreed to let us enter the marathon, providing we could get the payment through – and we were thankful for the use of another competitor's satellite phone. The organisers also let it slip that the storm meant a few competitors had pulled out. This meant we were in luck as we now had kit bags too! We'd managed it by the skin of our teeth and it was all on for the next morning!

As we made our way back to our hut, we were bouncing with excitement. Our guide couldn't believe we'd pulled it off – and neither could we. But, for now, it was time for some sleep.

PERSISTENCE

There are a few core values we choose to live by, the sort of values that have proven time and time again to be not only beneficial but essential for us to achieve the goals we set for ourselves and to get what we want out of life. One of these core values is persistence.

Having persistence can take you a long way in life, often pushing you beyond what you think you're capable of. Persistence is the opposite of giving up. When you are faced with setbacks, instead of calling it quits, persistence will keep you motivated to push on. It separates the determined from the quitters. It's what pushes people to reach their goals, striving for the top, and it's what can turn dreams into reality.

Think about many of the inspirational stories you have heard. The story of the chap who persisted through well over a thousand attempts before creating the light bulb (Thomas Edison), or the single mother living on a benefit, who persisted after numerous publishers rejected her manuscript, then went on to sell more than 120 million copies of *Harry Potter and the Philosopher's Stone* (J.K. Rowling). Then there's the man whose first business failed but he went on to build a computer software company worth billions of dollars (Microsoft's Bill Gates), and the woman who, after an incredibly tough childhood, never gave up on her dreams of becoming a broadcaster (Oprah Winfrey). What about that guy who refused to be drafted into the US Army, so was sentenced to jail and, because of that conviction, was banned from boxing for three years before his conviction was overturned, yet still went on to become the best boxer in the world? That man was Muhammad Ali.

What do these people all have in common? Persistence! It's hard to imagine any of them would have achieved what they did without persistence and the determination to never give up.

While these are some pretty extreme examples of what people can achieve, persistence is something you can apply in your day-to-day life. It isn't something that needs to be saved for an almighty battle to achieve something massive. It's something that can be applied in small ways every single day to allow you to get that one step closer to whatever you are striving for – no matter how big or small that thing might be.

Persistence can be used to keep you on track and to help you live each day the way you want to be living it. You might be striving to spend more time with your family, or maybe you're working towards getting a better job, one you will enjoy more, or maybe your goal is to live a healthier lifestyle, or to spend less time online and more time in the outdoors – whatever your goal is, persistence will help you get there. It will help you chip away at these things bit by bit until you have reached it.

There will always be challenges that pop up, things that test how much you want something and how hard you are willing to push to get it. Persistence will push you past those everyday obstacles, and it will help you to achieve your goals.

THE WORLD'S HIGHEST MARATHON

Chapter 4

The World's Highest Marathon

Mount Everest Base Camp to Namche Bazar

AMBER

The following morning, Serena and I were up bright and early as the marathon was due to start at 7 am and we still had to make our way back up to base camp. Despite the late night, we were ready and raring to go. At this time of year, the sun rises early on Everest and, by some unfathomable miracle, it was a beautiful, sunny day – an extreme contrast to the snowstorm we'd powered through the previous day. We were looking out at a clear blue sky. There wasn't a trace of a cloud on the brilliant blue horizon and the snow glistened as it melted in the already bright sunshine. The only sign of the destructive force of the previous day's weather was some remaining rubbish and the random pieces of tents scattered around. What we didn't know then was that this stunning weather would end up being a lot of people's undoing as the day wore on.

When we got to base camp, we said goodbye to our guide, who was going to meet us later in the day at Namche Bazar, then we paid some porters to take our packs down. The atmosphere hummed with excitement and there were lots of people rushing around. Race officials were doing last-minute preparations, and the organisers were talking over loudspeakers attempting to get everyone ready. There were nervous athletes (including us) stretching and warming up while waiting to find out which wave they would be in. We registered our race numbers, made sure all our gear was sorted and found out what wave we would start in.

With less than 10 minutes to go until the start of the race, reality started to sink in: What had we got ourselves into? While doing our final preparations, we chuckled back and forth anxiously, as the anticipation built. I could hardly contain my nerves.

Despite the possibility of the previous day's terrible weather continuing, we had come prepared for all weather conditions. We both started the race in leggings, t-shirts, running shoes, sunglasses and a hat. The sun is particularly harsh at altitude and being on snow meant the UV rays reflected back up from the white surface with full force. We had lathered ourselves in sun block, as we knew a sunny day like this was a recipe for sun stroke.

Shockingly, some of the athletes had started the race without sunglasses. I couldn't even open my eyes without sunglasses, so I was amazed that these athletes could actually see without them. Even this early in the morning, the glare was just too much. The snow was the brightest white to begin with, then the scorching sun beaming down on the harsh, white snow amplified the brightness so it felt as though my eyes would burn out if I looked at the ground too long without sunglasses.

We made our way to the start. Holy smokes, this was about to happen! We could barely contain our excitement. Our wave was up. We stepped up to the starting line and watched as a group of athletes took off down the snow in the wave of runners in front of us. We nervously chatted with the athletes on each side of us until the race official alerted everyone to get ready to start.

There were about 40 people in our wave, and we were all standing there, silent, at the starting line. We stood in slightly crouched positions with one leg in front of the other as we anticipated the sound of the starting gun. Serena and I looked at each other and grinned at the situation we had got ourselves into and then – bang!

The echo of the starting gun cracked with a ripple effect off the mountains surrounding us, and everyone took off at a full-blown sprint down the melting snow, all trying to get that step or two in front of the next person. Eventually, everyone slowed to their own pace and a few files formed. Serena and I started in the front half of the wave, but we were well aware of the 42 kilometres we still had to go.

I'm not sure if the race officials had anticipated a fresh dump of snow at this time of year. Looking down the mountain, we could see the wave of athletes in front of us all trying to navigate the slippery snow in their running shoes with zero traction. From our position, we could see what looked like doll-sized people below us, slipping and sliding, tripping and tumbling down the ice and rocks.

I took a deep breath as I braced myself for the inevitable and added to the chaos on the ice, as I struggled to stay upright while also attempting to run. The steep terrain and high altitude just topped things off – this was no easy challenge. When we fell over, it wasn't onto nice fluffy snow, as the trampling feet ahead of us had packed down the snow until it was rock hard; we fell, instead, onto hard ice that jarred us to the bone.

For the first few hours, we ran on the snow, or at least attempted to. It's probably more accurate to say we spent the first few hours dancing around struggling to keep upright, yet still falling over on the snow. Crampons or ice spikes would have been ideal, but in normal running shoes, we had no chance of staying on our feet.

What felt like masses of people poured down the slope with us, and we all tripped and slipped together, every which way on the way down. As I struggled along, I heard the crack of the starting gun for the wave behind us and I hoped like hell they wouldn't catch up and add to the chaos.

Looking down the slope, I could see the white blanket of snow was broken up by rocks, people and snow ledges that would be easy to slip off. I knew that if I slipped, I'd likely hurtle down until I hit a rock or a person, which did not look like fun. I saw a good few serious injuries occur early on, so I tried to have my wits about me, but I still managed a few hard tumbles and hit a lot of rocks.

To start with, we were on a wide-open ice field, which headed down sharply, funnelling into a steep gut that had rocks on each side and snow in the middle. The gut was a few football fields' long then it opened up onto a modest slope, which the trail cut across horizontally. This steep gut was a world of pain and, by watching other athletes stumble down in front of us as we ran, we got a little preview of what we were in for.

I had thought the best way to tackle it was to keep up the pace and beeline it straight down the middle because at least then I would land on snow and not rocks when I fell. I only made it a few metres into the gut before I slipped over and hit the ice with a hard crack to my tailbone that jarred my whole spine. That sure slowed me down!

With my tailbone throbbing, I tried to get back up and immediately slipped back over. It was impossible to stay on my feet. All around me, there were people on their hands and knees trying to make their way down. I was glad I wasn't the only one struggling. I looked across onto the other side of the gut and cracked up laughing as I noticed that Serena had just hit the deck as well. (It's always funny to see your sister falling over, right?)

I decided to try climbing down the rocks, so at least I'd have a little bit of grip on my shoes. Bad move again! I climbed onto the rocks and went to stand up as carefully as I could when, instantly, my feet flew out from underneath me.

The rocks had a layer of clear ice coating them, making this route just as slippery as the one across the snow, although this one being rocky meant it was slightly worse to land on.

Battered and bruised, I was starting to get frustrated and was aware that I still wasn't far into the race. The only way to get down the steepest parts was on my hands and knees, half crawling, half climbing and half slipping. I scurried down as quickly as possible, looking over at the poor critters who had already fallen and were waiting for the first aiders.

Going uphill or traversing across a slope on the snow was just as impossible as going downhill. It burnt a lot of energy trying to run up the hills with no traction, every step forward followed by half a step sliding backwards. Any time we traversed across a slope, we had to fight just to stay on the tilted, ice-packed trail. The effect of the high altitude was certainly noticeable. It felt like I was exercising with some sort of restrictive mask on, almost like trying to run while breathing through a straw – I couldn't take in enough oxygen to feel entirely comfortable.

After nearly two hours and having scrambled across a particularly nasty slope, I noticed that the ice was starting to thin out, and there were patches of mud and shrub punching through the snow. We were getting low enough now that the snow was starting to wither away.

The trail changed from snow to mud and rocks, and we were left navigating the uneven trail. We had to jump irregular, basketball-sized rocks, climb over bolders and negotiate all sorts of muddy pits and other obstacles in between. This made for an entertaining trail, but it also meant it wasn't possible to have a consistent stride, and I couldn't hit the trail at any sort of decent pace.

By early afternoon, the sun was high in the sky, striking us with the heat of all its bright rays, but the air was refreshingly icy, reminding us of the snow we had not long left. I had pulled away in front of Serena and we both set off at our own pace. It was a spectacular setting but hard going – nothing like a normal run at home on a nice tar-seal road with even footing and plenty of oxygen.

The challenging terrain demanded that I study the ground as I ran down the mountain. I couldn't let my concentration ease for even a moment. Having made it through the snow-covered part of the course, I hoped I was through the worst of it. It turned out I was, as the mud became dryer the further down I went.

I had thought I'd be able to let my legs take me down the trail almost in cruise control, but my legs fought the continuous tension of going downwards. Each time I got to the bottom of a dip, I welcomed the chance to use different leg muscles to head uphill. As I ran, I pondered over which was harder, the downhill or the uphill.

My ears were filled with the sound of my panting and I felt like I'd swallowed sandpaper. It was marvelous to be here on this mountain, even if my thighs and calves were burning and it took all my mental strength to keep my legs pumping away. My cheeks had turned rosy-red from the strenuous effort and sweat trickled down my back.

I got to the point on the steepest inclines where it was faster and took less effort to power walk rather than to keep jogging uphill. In my pouch, I was carrying two 500 ml bottles of water, which was a pretty insignificant amount, given how much liquid I was losing through sweat. I knew there were water top-up points along the route, so it was just a matter of not thinking about how dry my mouth was until then. This was easier said than done – it's usually the way, once you get extremely thirsty all you can think about is a sculling a cold glass of water!

As I continued onwards, I had no idea how much distance I had covered. After a good four hours of non-stop labouring, I started to convince myself I must be near the end, as I knew I could easily maintain a pace of 10 kilometres an hour even if I wasn't at my fittest. I had figured that if I could keep up the same pace as at home, it should take me four or five hours to do 42 kilometres. To that, I'd have to add on a bit of time to account for the terrain and the altitude, but I guess I hadn't anticipated how much.

When I came to an intersection, I could see some athletes turning and heading back up the mountain, while others were coming down. Surely it was only the mad buggers doing the ultra-marathon who were running back up the mountain, right?

Wrong. I was ushered to turn and head up the mountain and back up onto the snow once again! This was a blow to my morale as I realised I wasn't even close to the end. I had to laugh at how naïve I had been.

With my bottom lip dragging, I started pushing back up the mountain, then began the slippery, slidey run on the snow. It was a nasty, steep little section of the trail and it wasn't until almost an hour later, when I'd reached the top of the loop and started back downhill, that I had a smile back on my dial. Now I was on the home run … surely.

As I headed down the mountain and off the snow onto the muddy trail again, I passed the same intersection, quickly gulped down some water and refilled my water bottles before carrying on. My legs were growing heavy but, as I was lower down the mountain, I knew the hardest part was behind me. Ignoring my exhaustion, I was able to move a little more quickly now that the oxygen felt richer. I took in the stunning scenery of the mountains stretching as far as the eye could see.

I'd been going for well over seven hours when I came around a corner to see a bunch of race officials and local supporters on the trail. As I ran past, they yelled out that I had less than 6 kilometres to go and told me to make sure I grabbed my country's flag off the table just before the finish line. I hadn't known about this part – as we had entered the race at the last minute, there was probably a very slim chance they'd have two New Zealand flags there for us, but I was feeling optimistic.

The last hour had felt like double that; however, seeing the race officials reassured me that I was close to the end. I couldn't help but smile at the cheering each time I passed supporters. This gave me a new surge of energy, and I took off down the mountain, knowing the finish line was now in reach.

The day had worn on well into the afternoon and I kept my spirits high by focusing on the finish line. Dehydration was creeping in from the day's running and there was still plenty of heat in the afternoon sun, but now I had no trouble ignoring my craving for liquid as the end was so close. I crossed a small stream and started back up the other side when I made it to a table covered in the flags of all the countries that had runners in the race. There had to be more than 20 different flags on the table as there were a lot of different nationalities out there on the trail. I was absolutely stoked when I saw a stack of Kiwi flags! I hadn't expected that, but there must have been other runners out there representing New Zealand.

With a smile beaming across my face, I grabbed a New Zealand flag off the table, and the race officials gave me a big cheer and let me know the finish line was less than 1 kilometre away. I could hardly believe it, less than 1 kilometre – I was bubbling with excitement. It wasn't long before I could see the crowds of people in the distance. There were flags hanging down both sides of the trail, leading athletes towards the finish line.

At the finish line, supporters cheered as I ran under a huge arch and the timer stopped. My official time was eight hours, two minutes and 20 seconds. I had finished the world's highest marathon. It was an amazing feeling! I had an overwhelming sense of accomplishment in how far I'd managed to push myself. A finish-line marshal handed me a cold bottle of water and I wasted no time sculling back one bottle then sipping slowly on the next one while taking everything in.

About 20 minutes later, Serena came across the finish line with her flag. I found out I came 11th out of the female runners and 56th overall, with Serena coming in 13th woman and

64th overall. (And I beat Serena — I still haven't let her forget that.) Overall, not too bad for two Kiwis giving it a crack!

Serena was limping badly — not as a result of her falling over but because she's always suffered from bad knees. Her knee brace and Nurofen had not helped and, now that we had finished, we laughed as she told me she couldn't walk another step and I'd have to carry her down to the village. We'd both spent a bit more than eight hours running up and down the mountain that day. Some people might consider this to be eight hours of torture, but it was a beautiful day running through the Himalayas, which has to be one of the most scenic places you could go for a wee jog!

We were exhausted. Our whole bodies were fatigued and our legs felt like lead, yet we were on cloud nine. Our teeth chattered as the cold set in. Now that we were no longer running, my hands and feet had gone numb. Hobbling around the finishing area with our stiff legs seizing up, we watched more people come in. It was a great feeling knowing we had completed the challenge and we really enjoyed watching the triumph on other runners' faces as they crossed the finish line.

The fastest runner was a Nepalese man, Sudip Kulung, who had completed the race in just under four hours. How the heck he could run that fast over that terrain, I'll never know! I had assumed that, no matter how fit anyone was, the terrain would make running at speed impossible, but clearly not.

Local Nepalese runners took out all but three of the top 20 positions. They are an extremely tough bunch and I guess living at altitude on the rough terrain meant they were used to the conditions.

Later, we went back to our lodgings in Namche, where we had the unbelievable luxury of a warm shower. It was the first one we'd had since heading off on our hike more than a week before. We were lucky if the teahouses higher on the mountain had running water, let alone warm water for a shower.

Once we were warm and clean, I was tempted to jump into bed and rest my achy bones, but instead we headed to the lodge's common area to have a beer with some of the other marathoners. Although not all of the simple teahouses on Everest have running water, one thing they do all have in common is a supply of beer. Sinking a few bevvies, everyone shared the battles of their day. As we sat there warm and dry, enjoying the relaxing atmosphere, we heard there were still a few runners out there in the darkness. I couldn't imagine still being out there; just the thought of it made my legs ache. I had to admire their determination in pushing on to reach their goal. It would have taken a hell of a lot of mental strength to still be attempting to finish after dark.

The next day, we looked at all the sorry sods around us. Everyone was still beaming with pride and accomplishment but there were some seriously damaged bodies, mostly as a result of the beautiful weather. With the blizzard the day before the marathon, not many people had expected the intense sun to be out, so they wore little or no sun protection. On top of that, the reflection of the sun bouncing off the snow amplifies its burning strength, so you get burnt a heck of a lot more than normal. That day, I saw some of the most severely sunburnt people I'd ever seen. Their whole faces looked like they had been caught in a fire and badly burnt. Some of them had to seek medical attention and others couldn't move their legs or arms as their skin had been pulled so tight by the severe sunburn.

We also found out that some runners had suffered snow blindness. I thought back to some of the athletes I'd noticed not wearing sunglasses at the start. Snow blindness is caused by the sun's UV rays reflecting off the snow then burning the cornea in the eye, which can result in temporary blindness. This loss of vision had such a sudden effect on some athletes that they had to stop and sit down until the medics caught up to them and led them to the nearest village. Luckily for them, the damage to their eyes wasn't permanent – they just had to rest in a dark room until they got their eyesight back.

We met up with our guide in Namche, and he greeted us with a big grin and a cheerful pat on the back. He was almost more excited than we were when he heard we'd finished the race. Together, we set off back down the trail towards Lukla, from where we were due to fly back to Kathmandu. We'd originally planned to make our way down the mountain more slowly, but the marathon saw us coming down sooner than we'd planned.

Even after a night's sleep, my body had not fully recovered and my knees did not like my weighty pack, but the hike was mostly downhill and there was no rush to get to the finish line. We made it to Lukla early in the afternoon and spent the rest of the day relaxing before our flight the next day.

That evening, we sat in a small Nepalese restaurant, sipping on orange tea and marvelling at the twists and turns our trip had taken. Getting to base camp at the exact time of the marathon was too much of a coincidence for us not to seize the opportunity. It had certainly added to the adventure and, as we sat there, we began to ponder what our next adventure might be.

TAKING ON CHALLENGES

AMBER

Taking on a challenge is something that usually requires deliberate action and effort to push yourself past what is normal for you. It means taking on something that isn't easy in order to achieve your goals. It can take a few attempts to conquer a challenge, which isn't a bad thing – after all, if it wasn't hard to begin with, then it probably wasn't a challenge in the first place.

Regularly, challenges have low points that may have you swearing to yourself, 'Never, ever again', but in your pursuit, you will learn and become stronger, and this will help you to overcome obstacles to get what you want out of life. Once you have proved to yourself that you can do anything you put your mind to, that low point will seem insignificant, while your sense of accomplishment will have you chasing more challenges.

Some of the unexpected hurdles can be fun and exciting, while others might be frustrating and time consuming, requiring a lot more effort than you anticipated. Often, overcoming the tough hurdles brings you the most satisfaction as you push on and, eventually, achieve your goal.

A good portion of the time, things aren't easy and you'll need persistence to reach whatever it is you are striving for. If you don't succeed straightaway, try going about things in different ways in order to make that necessary breakthrough.

Challenges are there to test how much you really want something, and it can be empowering to view them as a chance to get something more out of life. That night at Mount Everest base camp, Serena and I could have accepted that we were too late to enter the marathon, but we knew this was something we really wanted to do, so we persisted to make it happen. We challenged ourselves, not knowing if we could run a marathon in tough conditions and, in doing so, we not only had a once-in-a-lifetime experience but were also rewarded with the achievement of proving to ourselves that we really could do it.

If things don't work out the way you planned, keep the goal but adapt and change the plan for achieving it. Remember, a challenge is all about giving it a go – it's not supposed to be easy; the more you fight for it, the closer you will get!

AN
UNEXPECTED
SETBACK

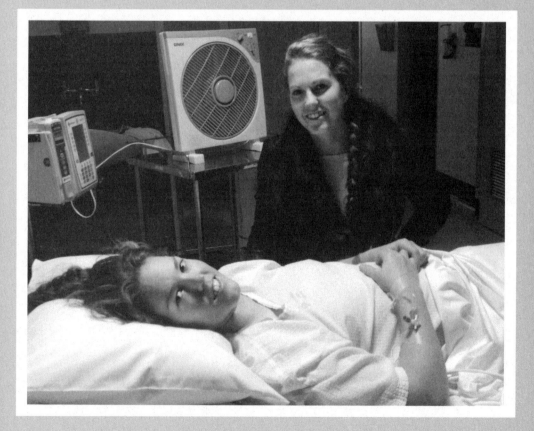

Chapter 5

An Unexpected Setback

Australia, New Zealand and Alaska, USA

SERENA

The cool air felt good rushing past my face as I flew down the white-blanketed mountain on my snowboard, carving in and out but also a tad out of control, which was half the fun of it. It was pretty normal for me to be slightly out of control on my first few runs as I hadn't been on a snowboard in more than a year. My partner, Atoni, and I were taking a break from our jobs in the mines of Western Australia to enjoy an action-packed holiday at a ski-field in Victoria.

This was Atoni's first time snowboarding, so I ran him through the basics – after giving him a few amateur pointers, he was away. For a first timer, he picked it up rather quickly, although he still had a little bit of work to do in perfecting a controlled stop, which provided some great entertainment for me.

After the first few rusty runs down the mountain, my muscle memory came flooding back. It felt natural again and I was back in control and having loads of fun. We spent a few days having a blast on our snowboards, doing all the runs down the mountain multiple times. We also had a ball mucking around in the tricks park, sliding on the rails and getting a little air time on the jumps, which sometimes ended with us both in hysterics if one of us landed in a bit of a sprawl.

The weather was threatening to pack it in for the day, and the indecisive wind blew thick, white patches of mist across the mountain, so conditions kept going in and out of white-out. However, the few clear patches meant it was still good enough to make the most of the afternoon. With my confidence up, I started hitting the bigger jumps and, after roughly landing a few flips, I was eager to perfect my landings.

Having an absolute blast, I headed down another run in the tricks park, lining up my snowboard for the jump on the right this time. The moment I sped onto the ramp to make the jump, I knew I wasn't going to make a clean landing. I hesitated for a split second, which was all it took for me to come off the ground at slightly the wrong angle. I went for the backflip anyway, figuring I would land in a sprawl like I had the few other times I'd misjudged my landings. I was moving with a lot more speed this time, but I was committed. It was too late to pull out — I was already in the air. Sure enough, my landing was all wrong. There was a loud thud as I hit the ground hard, tumbled onto my back and then slid along the solid packed ice until I came to a grinding halt.

The wind had been knocked out of me. I lay on my back for a few moments gasping to get my breath back. After what felt like a good few minutes of trying to regain myself, I tried to get up but I couldn't quite muster the strength as my breath had not returned. I was still wheezing hard, trying to suck some air into my lungs. Something felt odd, almost fuzzy, but I couldn't put my finger on it. I thought, 'Wow, I must have hit hard this time …'

For a moment I stopped struggling to get up, and worked on controlling my breathing, trying to slowly inhale and exhale, eagerly waiting for a surge of strength to come back. As I lay there in the snow, I tried to ignore the small thought in the back of my mind about how good the ice-cold snow felt on a section of my back. I had yet to connect the dots with the increasing pain to that section of my back. I thought, 'Strange, I'm still winded, why can't I get my breath back?'

It had been a long time since I had been properly winded, so I wondered if I had just forgotten what it felt like. Finally, after what seemed like forever, with a slow, deep inhale and exhale, I managed to get my breathing under control. I tried again to stand … nothing. My body would not respond. A flash of panic flickered through me as I recognised the excruciating pain in my back I had been ignoring.

Almost as quickly as the panic came, it was gone as I squashed any worst-case-scenario thoughts that were attempting to push their way into my head. 'She'll be right!' I thought, a phrase that is in regular use in Amber's and my vocabulary. This phrase usually brings a bit of humour into a situation and can often lighten the mood. More importantly, it is a positive way of reminding ourselves that everything is going to be OK, in the end.

As the adrenaline began to wear off, pain gripped the middle and upper sections of my back. It felt like my spine was in a vice, being twisted tighter and tighter. Even at a distance, Atoni could tell there was something wrong. Usually, I would be up after a few seconds, laughing away at having fallen, so Atoni knew that if I was still on the ground after this long, it wasn't good news.

He came over and asked if I was OK. I was glad to see his face from my stranded position, but I was too confused to give him any information that would help. I tried to crack a smile but he could see I was in agony. Having checked in with me, he assured me he'd be back soon, then rushed off to the nearest ski hut to get help.

While he was gone, I lay there, calmly looking up at the clouds. Still unsure what the problem was, I could feel the soothing cold ice attempting to numb my pain.

The next thing I knew, unfamiliar sets of hands were shuffling me onto a stretcher and I was lifted off the ground and placed in a sled. As I was a first responder as part of my job, everything was familiar and I felt like I was watching them work with interest, although this was the first time I had been on the receiving end of treatment.

The stretcher was strapped onto the back of the snowmobile, and I heard the motor start. After a rough ride skating over the snow on the back of a snowmobile, I was loaded into a field ambulance that took me to the ski-field's medical centre.

As I lay on the stretcher, I was greeted by another stranger in a uniform and he started to go through all sorts of familiar tests. A few hours of X-rays and assessments later, I was still no closer to knowing what was going on.

'Well, they haven't given me any bad news after the X-ray, so it must just be something like torn ligaments,' I said to Atoni, optimistically.

He managed to conceal his concern, but he had telltale signs of deep worry across his face.

I wondered how long torn ligaments would take to recover from, as I was loving the challenge of CrossFit and didn't want to have to take too much time away from it.

The doctor decided I needed to get to the orthopaedic ward in a Melbourne hospital. A bumpy ambulance ride and a helicopter flight later, I made it there in the very late evening. Although the pain was right up there and threatened to take over completely, I did my best to disregard it and declined pain relief. I wanted to have a clear mind to be able to give the doctor as accurate a description as possible of my back pain. Who knows, the pain might have dulled down and it might just have been a simple strain – I was still hopeful.

I thought I was holding it together fine over my journey to the hospital, but my pain must have been too obvious for the helicopter paramedic to ignore. He ignored my half-hearted protests and administered some pain relief. It was a much better helicopter ride after that!

By midnight, I was lying on a bed in the emergency ward awaiting the results of a whole lot of tests that involved plenty of poking and prodding and a few more X-rays. I was alone, as Atoni wasn't allowed to accompany me in the helicopter. I had feeling in my toes, which was a great sign, but I couldn't get up. I was still optimistic but slowly starting to come to terms with the fact that things were slightly worse than I'd hoped.

Atoni arrived during the night after making the five-hour drive from the ski-field. He'd probably had a worse time than me up until now as he'd had to pack up our gear and drive into the city, all while being so worried about me.

In the early hours of the morning the doctor arrived and delivered the devastating news that this was not a sprain. Two of my vertebrae were broken, and there was a partial break in a third vertebra. He said I was very lucky not to have spinal cord damage and that the muscles in my back had held everything together extremely well considering the high-impact trauma it had received. Even so, I had to have surgery as soon as possible, and the doctor warned me there was a real possibility I might not be able to walk again.

Even though the news had not yet sunk in, I instinctively knew it was important to stay positive. I knew it wouldn't help if I started to think down the dark tunnel of the negative impact this could have on my life. This tested me hugely – the the darkness of what this could mean kept trying to creep into my mind, but I refused to let it take hold. I was determined to believe the worst-case scenario was *not* an option for me. No matter how long it took and how hard it would be, I was prepared to make sure I would make a full recovery. After all, she'll be right!

Amber made the flight over from the other side of Australia that morning and backed me up with the same 'she'll be right' attitude until I was whisked away to surgery.

Bolts, screws and titanium plates later, I woke up from surgery, wiggled my toes and – with a smile – I knew everything was going to be OK and life was good. Atoni and Amber were with me in the hospital, and Mum and Dad were on their way from New Zealand. I was very lucky to have such amazing support.

From the moment I woke up that morning, I was eager to get moving and test my body. Although still cautious, I was bursting with impatience and felt up to the task of attempting to take a step or two. Though the doctors had been reluctant at first, they said that if I were up to it and wanted to give it a go, it was good to get moving to start the recovery process. The sooner the better, I reckoned.

That very day, with Amber egging me on and Atoni's encouragement, and with the doctors' and nurses' assistance, I struggled out of bed and took my first few steps. There was a lot of pain and plenty of sharp stabs in my back, but I made it down the corridor and back incredibly slowly. This gave me an assurance that I would eventually get my normal life back. I felt as though I had just summited a mountain. I knew attitude was everything, and by staying positive and working hard, I would claw my way back to a full recovery. Each day from there on, I slowly got better and better. Five or so days later, I was well enough – with assistance – to check out of hospital and make the flight back to Perth.

Once I got back to the real world, I had a few setbacks that tried to chip away at my positive outlook. I was hit with the hefty ambulance bill and an astronomical helicopter bill as a result of my accident. Then, once I had recovered enough to work and had passed a physical, I was still denied the chance to return to work in the mines because of the seriousness of my injury – and no one could tell me how long that would be for. The income insurance I had been paying for years all of a sudden deemed me ineligible to claim anything, and the company chose to return my contributions rather than covering my income while I was unable to work. To top it off, although I worked and paid tax in Australia, I was not eligible to be covered by Medicare, and because I was working in Australia, I was not eligible for help from ACC in New Zealand either. I wasn't able to be treated like a resident in either country.

Not being able to earn an income made it pretty hard to cover my normal living expenses, which were greatly increased by the medical bills, then the rehab would be next. Because my accident had happened on the other side of Australia from where I was living, I must have slipped through the cracks; I never heard from the specialists, doctors or physios who would usually help people through recovery and offer guidance after surgery. So I decided I would get on with my recovery myself and do what I thought would help.

The mental battle of recovery can certainly be a tough one. It was pretty rough getting hit with so many mental and physical battles all at once. Aside from the stress of how I was going to make it all work, it was very tough not being able to do the physical things I was used to doing.

At the beginning, simple tasks like getting dressed and showering took time and effort. I was fit and loved being active, yet every time I tried to do anything, I couldn't. I wanted to go back to the gym, and get back outdoors to go on adventures, but even little things were out of my reach. I had to build my way back up from ground level, which was disheartening at times. However, I never took my mind off the overall goal of full recovery, and I would push past the down times by just getting on with it. Amber and Atoni helped a lot through this time and I had great support from family and the friends I was flatting with.

I didn't want to dwell on any of my setbacks and was constantly reminding myself I had to look at the bright side – I could still walk, I was in good health and I was going to make sure I made a full recovery.

I had been going to the local CrossFit gym for a couple of years and had made some really great friends there. Amazingly, they banded together to raise money to help me out. I was blown away when they raised over a thousand dollars for my recovery, which I am still truly humbled by today. It was unbelievable to me that this small CrossFit team could raise so much and that they had done it all for me.

To some of the members, I was a stranger, yet they had still donated. It certainly helped knowing there are such kind and caring people in this world.

I couldn't afford to wait around for work that I may or may not get cleared to do; I knew I had to adapt to my situation and do something different. I decided that I had to move back home to New Zealand where I could start over in something fresh. There, I would be able to start my own business and I could work while I was still on the recovery road. Though this was the best thing for me, Atoni had a great job in the mines and we didn't want to jeopardise that. I couldn't sit around cooped up all day, but I didn't want Atoni to sacrifice his career because I'd decided to go back to New Zealand. It was a hard decision to return home without my partner, but we knew it was the only way we could both move forward in our careers. Together, we decided it would be for the best if we had a long-distance relationship while I figured out if I could create a successful business in New Zealand.

During the previous four years, Amber and I had spent many hours together in Perth planning several businesses. Twice we became extremely close to taking the plunge before our due diligence uncovered a detail that made us think better of it. The work we'd done earlier helped prepare me to take the leap on starting my own business in New Zealand while I recovered.

Over the years, our parents successfully developed and expanded their own businesses, so moving back home meant I had them for counsel. This was a great benefit – being new to business I learnt *and still do learn* a lot from them. Before long, I'd gone into a partnership with my father and I set up and started running my own glam camping business.

Before my accident, Amber and I had loosely planned our next adventure. We were set on doing a mountaineering expedition and we liked the idea of climbing one of the seven summits – the highest mountains on each of the seven continents. My accident threw a spanner in the works, and choosing the highest mountain on a continent probably wasn't the best place to start after a broken spine.

When I moved back to New Zealand, Amber decided it was time to leave the mines and headed to the USA to work. I couldn't let her have all the adventures, so we decided to stick with our planned mountaineering trip.

With Amber already in America, we settled on a trip to Alaska to climb Mount McKinley, which is also known as Denali. At 6194 metres high, the mountain is the highest in North America. Many mountaineers climb it on their quest to climb the seven summits and, of the seven mountains, only Asia's Mount Everest and South America's Mount Aconcagua are higher.

I had eight months from when I broke my back until I had to be fully recovered in order to make the climb in April 2015. Not only did I need to be fully recovered and able to do everything normally again, but I would also need to be trained and ready to carry a 40-kilogram pack and tow a 50-kilogram sled for three weeks up a tough mountain, known for its extreme weather conditions. I knew the dates were a little tight with my recovery; however, having a goal to work towards gave me added strength and enthusiasm.

The climb was going to be my motivation and a massive goal for me to work hard towards. Amber was as invested as I was in my recovery. She would call or message me when she could from the other side of the world, egging me on and making sure I was on track for my recovery. If I was not ready in eight months, I was going to have to pull out and I refused to consider that as a viable option.

After my accident, I started out very slowly with my recovery and began just walking to a park near where I lived. It felt very odd, as if the muscles on my back swung loosely, no longer connected to anything. I slowly improved with each walk I went on and worked my way back into CrossFit, going easy at the start and working my way up until I could lift decent weights above my head again.

When I moved back to New Zealand, I scrambled together some workout gear so I could do workouts at home, and I started hiking up hills carrying a backpack. Gradually, I increased the weight of my hiking pack until I could carry 50 kilograms – this was more than I needed, but I wanted to be sure. Then I added an altitude mask to the mix to really ramp things up.

Eventually, after months of consistent hard work around a busy time of starting my own business, I'd reached my goal of recovery and finally felt like myself again. I would be meeting Amber in America to make our way to Alaska in order to embark on an epic mountaineering expedition, and we had even planned a warm-up climb on Mount Baker, about 200 kilometres from Seattle, Washington.

When Your Twin Sister is in Trouble

AMBER

I was in the red-dirt outback of Western Australia, halfway through a two-week shift working in the gold mines. After a long 12-hour shift and a quick workout in the gym, I had showered and was grabbing a bite to eat at the mess before I hit the hay. I had just sat down with my plate of food when I felt a dull ache in the centre-top section of my back. I thought it was a bit strange but brushed it off, thinking maybe I'd tweaked it in the gym without realising it. I was fit as a fiddle and never really had an injury from the gym, but I couldn't think what else it could have been from.

By the time I got back to my room and was ready for bed, the dull ache in my back had increased considerably. I didn't think much of it, as I tried to recall something I'd done earlier that could have caused it.

A few hours later, I woke from a deep sleep with a sore back and the feeling something was wrong, but I couldn't put my finger on it. Less than half an hour later, my phone rang. It was Atoni calling from the other side of Australia. Straight away, I knew it wasn't going to be good news. He filled me in on what had happened. He said Serena needed surgery as soon as they could fit her in and the doctors had said there was a possibility she might be unable to walk again.

I was absolutely crushed. Serena was my partner in crime, my other half, my adventure double. The thought of her even having the slightest chance of not walking again was totally and utterly devastating.

I hung up the phone and sat there in stunned silence. Suddenly, it clicked. That strange sore back I'd had for no reason that evening … it was the same section of the back that Serena had broken. It made total sense to me now. This wasn't the first time we had felt each other's pain, and I was annoyed I hadn't clicked earlier – not that there was anything I could have done about it, I guess.

The next morning, I took the first flight out of the mines, then the next flight across Australia to Melbourne. I had gone over many different scenarios in my head but decided that there was only one possible outcome – Serena would have to work incredibly hard and put all her might into making a full recovery; it was the only option I could accept. Not that I'd tell her this, but she's bloody tough physically and even tougher mentally, so this would just be her next challenge to tackle. I would be there to make sure it happened and to give her a little push if and when it was needed.

Walking into the hospital, not quite knowing what to expect, I felt horrible. To my shock but absolute delight, Serena was in good spirits. How the hell she could be so positive so soon after something like this happening, I'll never know. I guess she had already come to the same conclusion I had – there is nothing to gain from dwelling on the past and the only way forward was for her to tackle this new challenge.

I was relieved when she got out of surgery and the doctors said everything had gone really well. It took a while for her to come to, and we were soon bickering about the unfair advantage she now had over me as I joked she was part bionic with all the screws and bolts holding her back together.

That very day, not long after surgery and still in her bandages, Serena took her first steps. I was blown away by her determination and could hardly believe she was walking down the corridor so soon after surgery. I was over the moon for her, and I knew then that she was going to do everything in her power to make a full recovery. With a little bit of egging on and some hard work, I was confident we would be back to being partners in crime tackling new adventures in no time. I also knew it would be a rough and bumpy road to recovery, but she was determined as hell and wouldn't give herself any other option.

A few days later, she was checking out of hospital, ready to tackle a slow but steady recovery. As Atoni and I wheeled Serena down the hospital hallway in her wheelchair to check out, the doctor chatted, saying that this was probably a bit of a wake-up call for Serena to slow down with the adventures and take things easy. I pondered over this for the whole flight back to Perth. It turned out Serena had been thinking about the same thing. We agreed that the doctors had all been absolutely amazing but, on this particular issue, the doctor had been totally wrong.

Slow down? Slow down on adventures? A wake-up call to slow down?

Serena and I had independently come to the same conclusion: if anything, this was a wake-up call to speed up. We realised how short life is and how your whole life can change in an instant. We realised we needed to make the most of everything and get out there and do as many of the things we wanted to do as possible, because who knows if or when we wouldn't be able to do those things. We had a whole new appreciation of life, health and wellbeing and we weren't about to sit around and waste it. We certainly weren't about to slow down …

In fact, during Serena's recovery, we started to plan our next adventure – climbing Denali in Alaska. This gave Serena something to strive for, a little fuel for the fire on top of the challenge of recovery. I knew mountaineering on one of the seven summits was going to be tough adventure for me, and I was in full health! So, I couldn't imagine what it would be like for someone recovering from a broken spine. That said, there was only one way to find out and find out we did.

When we had finally made it to Alaska and stood at the base of Denali, we were both a little nervous, but I was calmed when I could see Serena was ready to tackle this mountain with a vengeance. To her, this mountain was the last hurdle to getting over her injury and we both knew it would be a fierce hurdle at that.

We soon found that *fierce* was an understatement when it came to describing the ascent. We battled -40°C temperatures and 145-kilometre per hour winds, all while carrying 30-kilogram packs and towing 50-kilogram sleds. We fought through blizzards and snowstorms, made ice caves to seek shelter, scaled ice walls on fixed ropes and went through countless days of numb noses, feet and hands, not knowing if we had succumbed to frostbite yet.

The weather was so bad for the three weeks we spent

on the mountain that when it was time to make our final push up the mountain, 6190 metres above sea level, we were forced to turn back. Only one person made it to the top in the 21 days we were there, yet, sadly, he never made it back down the mountain.

Despite not summiting, we were able to walk away safely, feeling accomplished at having given it our best shot, learning valuable lessons about ourselves after we'd been pushed to our limits.

DON'T HOLD BACK

SERENA

After my accident, a lot of people thought I would slow down my adventuring. Always meaning well, they'd say things like, 'You must have learnt your lesson', and ask if I planned to take it easy. I sure had learnt my lesson – how easily things can change! I learnt that I'm not bulletproof and that things can be taken away in the blink of an eye.

However, they were wrong in thinking that this would mean I'd slow down. In fact, what I took from this lesson was the exact opposite: I learnt that I had to live every minute to the fullest, to take every opportunity and to explore everything I could. I had to chase my dreams and do everything I wanted to do, not letting anything hold me back, least of all fear.

If the worst had happened and I had no longer been able to walk, I believe I would have looked back and been thankful for all the adventures I had experienced. But if I had been too fearful to have gone on all those adventures, I believe I would have looked back with a little regret and said, 'Why didn't I do more? Why did I not do all those things I'd always wanted to?'

Nobody talks about the mountains they didn't climb (whether it be a physical or metaphorical mountain), and nobody talks about the adventures they didn't have and the experiences they didn't live. These adventures and experiences enrich our lives and, even when we feel fear, we need to go out and climb that mountain anyway. No matter what your mountain might be, life should be lived. After all, there is no point tip toeing through life only to arrive safely at death.

ALASKAN HUSKIES AND DOG SLEDDING

Chapter 6

Alaskan Huskies and Dog Sledding

Michigan, USA

AMBER

I had just taken the plunge and committed to spending a very cold winter working in Michigan. I was taking on a brand-new job, one a little out of the box: I was going to be a dog-sledding tour guide (musher is the proper term). I was picturing I was going to be just like one of those people I had seen in the movies who drives a sled being pulled along by a team of huskies through the snowy mountains. I may not have had any dog-sledding experience, or dog-handling experience in general, but I love animals and knew I would love the job, so I wasn't about to let that minor detail stop me.

I applied for and got the job at the kennels where our younger sister, Jasmine, had worked the previous year. Once I heard that I'd got the job, I beavered away for months to get a working visa while packing up my life in Perth.

Around the time Serena moved back to New Zealand to recuperate after her back injury, I headed to Michigan, where it was autumn. This gave me a few weeks to get my bearings and learn the ground and the many trails before the winter snow covered them over completely. The place where I was working was the real McCoy. It was way out in the woods in the middle of nowhere. In a clearing in the woods stood a cabin, which was totally off-grid. There were solar-power cells and battery banks to run the cabin's electrics, and there was a back-up generator for when the snow was heavy and there wasn't enough sun. Most of the cooking was done over a fire, and the stove was used only on the odd occasion when we could spare our limited power. There was no TV, barely any phone reception and pretty much no technology whatsoever. It was perfect!

Beside the cabin were rows of kennels, which were home to all the dogs. And there were a lot of dogs – 125 Alaskan huskies in total, and we sure knew about it when 125 dogs got excited and started barking all at once. Thankfully, they all had name tags on their kennels, otherwise, in the beginning, I would have had a tough time working out who was who.

The owners, a lovely couple who absolutely loved dogs, lived and breathed dog sledding even after having done it for many years. Aside from the owners, it was me and one other guide, a girl who had arrived shortly after me, looking after all these dogs until three or four more guides arrived later in the season. We sure had our work cut out for us in the meantime.

Out of these adorable but slightly intimidating huskies, I was dedicated my own team of 25, which I would stick with for the season, but I still trained and worked with all the dogs. Being a musher was as epic as I'd imagined it would be and it did not disappoint in terms of adventure. As there was no snow yet, we ran the dogs using a four-wheel motorbike in place of a sled. The set-up was exactly the same as with a sled, but the dogs pulled the musher on the quad bike across dirt trails instead of a sled over snow. With the quad bike, I'd use the brakes to stop the eager dogs from pulling once we'd halted, but later, when we were working in snow with a sled, I'd dig my snow hook into the snow to act like an anchor. The hook was roped to the sled, and the harder the dogs pulled, the more the hook would dig into the snow, preventing them from taking off again.

We'd take our teams out on a 3- to 8-kilometre run early each day, before it got too warm for them. As the dogs were used to running in the snow, we ran them in the cool of the morning to avoid any risk of them overheating in autumn. Hooking up a team of huskies involved wrestling each dog into a harness as they wiggled and jumped around, raring to go. I'd then attach them to the gang line in pairs to make two columns. A gang line runs down the middle of the rows and is then attached to the sled or quad bike. On the gang line, there are two columns of dogs – the left side and the right side – so they run in pairs, one beside the other.

The number of dogs attached at one time depended on how well a musher could control their dogs and how fast the musher wanted them to go. Six dogs is fairly typical for a sled but we could run between six and 14 dogs at once with the quad bike. The more dogs there are, the harder and faster they can pull, and the stickier the situation would get if something went wrong.

The front two dogs are the lead dogs, the important ones who lead the team and would react to my commands and steer the team where I wanted them to go. The back two dogs are called the wheel dogs, and they generally take more of the weight, so that was where I put the big guys or the ones I knew would pull really hard.

As we attached each dog to the sled or quad bike, the excitement of going out on a run would spread through the kennel like wildfire and almost instantly the rest of the 125 dogs were all barking like crazy in thrilled anticipation that their run might be next. These dogs just love to run. I've heard some people question if the dogs like running and pulling sleds – I can confirm that these huskies absolutely loved it as it gave them purpose. They were no different to most dogs at home; the minute you say 'Walk?', they start wagging their tails and happily jumping up and down eager to get out on a walk. The minute these huskies knew they would be heading out on a run, it was hard to contain their energy.

This passion for running proved challenging any time I halted the team, or at the start of a run while I connected the dogs to the gang line. The sled or quad bike had to be tied to a pole if I was in the kennel, or a tree if I were out on a trail in the woods. This was the only way to stop the dogs from taking off early without their musher – me.

In the kennel, once I completed attaching the team I would give the 'Ready' signal, and simultaneously pull the quick release on the rope, releasing the team, already fizzing and ready to take off as fast as they could. After a few practice runs and training sessions with the owners, I had picked things up pretty quickly and they were happy for me to take the reins and start mushing on my own.

There are a number of main commands to mush a dog sled team. First was a high-pitched 'Ready' to perk up the dogs' ears and get them paying attention in anticipation to start a run. With this command, some dogs would start lunging forwards, eager to take off while others would turn around and watch my face expectantly as they waited for the next command to come out of my mouth.

'Ready' was followed by 'Let's go!' and a simultaneous pull of the quick release, their cue it's go-time. They would take off like sprinters after the starting gun, their powerful strides jerking the sled from its static position. During the run, yelling 'Haaa!' in a deep voice would signal the lead dogs to turn left, while yelling 'Geee!' in a high-pitched voice told them to turn right.

To get them to slow down, I'd yell 'Whooa!' in a deep, soothing voice, while I put some weight on the brake pad. Unlike the snow hook, which acted like an anchor to halt the dogs, the brake pad was a rubber mat that dragged along the ground between the two skis on the sled that I stood on. The mat was between my feet, so it was easy to rest a foot on it in order to slow down my team. The more weight I put on it, the more resistance it created, making the dogs slow down. An extended 'Whooooa, whooooa, whooa!' would tell the team to stop completely, then I'd dig my snow hook into the snow to keep them from taking off again.

It took me a while to get to know each of my dogs' individual traits, and they certainly tested me by choosing their own commands at the beginning. Some of them were so cunning, they could pick when a newbie musher was in charge, then they'd see just how much they could get away with. It wasn't long before these dogs caught on that I wasn't going to be letting them get away with anything. Despite this, I formed a tight bond with each of them. I soon figured out which dogs were best at what positions and each of their strong points.

I must admit, I did get in a few pickles though. Out on a run one autumn morning, I had my quad bike brakes jammed on trying to halt the team, and the cheeky little buggers kept lunging forwards not wanting to stop. Bit by bit, lunge by lunge, they managed to keep the bike nudging forwards and up onto a bank while I was still on it. Well, one side of the bike went up the waist-high bank anyway and the other side stayed on flat ground. It all happened in slow motion and was almost comical as I could see exactly what was about to happen, but there was nothing I could do to stop it.

I launched off the bike as it rolled and I landed on the ground with a thud. I had half a second to jump out of the bike's way before it landed on the exact same spot where I had just been sprawled out moments before. The dogs stood there oblivious to the situation and looked back impatiently at me and the upside-down bike, as if this were a very inconvenient interruption to their run. I thought I had a pretty slim chance of getting the bike back on its wheels, but I managed to heave it back over, no sweat, and off we trotted.

In addition to sussing out the dogs, it took a little while for me to get to know the dozens of trails running through the woods – it was like a rabbit warren and each one seemed identical. I'm usually pretty good at getting orientated and finding my way around in remote places, but this wasn't straight forward. The woods looked the same in every direction, there were barely any clues, no landmarks to go off, the flat terrain rarely changed and the sun hardly came out to help me keep my bearings.

Before I knew it, autumn was over and the winter snow set in. Everything turned fairy-tale white in the woods and we were in season – but, boy was it cold! When I say it was a cold winter in Michigan, I mean it was an unbelievably, bone-chillingly, hand-numbingly freezing cold. I would stare in disbelief at the temperature gauge when it read -30°C. I couldn't even imagine how cold a wind chill of -50°C would be until I got here and experienced it for myself.

The minute I walked outside, my eyelashes would freeze instantly, making it look like I was wearing thick, white mascara, and any hair sticking out from my beanie froze instantly, turning it white and crunchy with frost, even though it was dry to begin with. It was crazy to walk outside and have something freeze within seconds. By far, these were the coldest conditions I had ever been in, and I had committed to working a full winter in these conditions, a full winter working outside in the elements. A good thing about Michigan's cold weather was that it was a dry cold, and it was rarely windy, so this made a big difference to the pleasantness of the outdoors.

I found working with the huskies really rewarding and fulfilling. I became especially attached to my team of 25 huskies, but I spent a lot of time training and working with all 125 of them. I learnt every dog's name and came to understand their individual traits, habits, gaits and a whole lot of other little quirks about them. Soon, I knew who the lead dogs were, who the feisty ones I needed to keep an eye on were, who started the fights, who the work horses were and who were the fakers pretending to pull. I knew which dogs didn't like running next to each other, which dogs where good at teaching the younger ones and which dogs were mischief.

I had the most amazing winter taking tourists on dog-sled tours. Guests could choose a half-day or full-day tour, which was either a 15-kilometre or 30-kilometre experience sledding through the woods, stopping in the snow to take in the winter wonderland.

Some of the really keen tour groups would come out on an overnight trip: we'd spend the day sledding through the woods and stop in at a tiny wooden cabin before nightfall. The cabin was very basic and just big enough for a few bunk beds and a fireplace. After lighting the fire for my guests, setting up the dogs on straw beds with warm meat soup for dinner, we all sat around the campfire laughing and chatting while we cooked dinner over the fire and roasted marshmallows. The nights in the cabin were usually freezing, as the fireplace barely provided any warmth, so we always made sure our guests brought plenty of warm gear. This meant it was easy to get up in the mornings, as we didn't have the comfort of a warm bed to get out of. In the morning, we had breakfast over the campfire before heading back through the woods to the kennels.

As well as working hard during the season taking paying guests dog sledding, I also spent a lot of time training up a separate race team – a bunch of the biggest, baddest, strongest dogs. I would take them out on long runs for conditioning as I was training them for a race at the end of the season. Most guides don't get this sort of opportunity; however, I was super keen, persistent and happy to put in the hard yards when everyone else would be inside keeping warm. I was absolutely thrilled to get such a rare opportunity.

Training the race team wasn't easy. On top of my normal day-to-day workload, which was full of physical jobs such as shovelling snow and chopping firewood when I wasn't sledding, I spent a lot of time with my race team, taking them on 7- to 10-hour runs in all weather conditions, standing on my race sled, with numb hands and feet and freezing my butt off in the sub-zero conditions. Race sleds are a third of the size and 10 times more fun than tour sleds. They are narrower, faster and more flexible, which also means they are much easier to roll and fall off of.

A normal training run for my race team would be around a hundred kilometres, and every one of them was remarkable, containing something different to entertain me. Even when my race team threw challenges at me, or I got miserably cold for hours on end, this was quickly counteracted by my love of being out in the woods with nothing but nature all around, either in beautiful sunshine or with magical snowflakes attempting to freeze my eyes shut. How grand life was!

One of my first long training runs with my race team was also one of the most challenging. Early one morning, I picked 10 huskies out of my race team, wrestled them into their harnesses and hooked them up to my sled, ready for a hundred-kilometre training run.

My breath frosted in front of me with each exhale, and snowflakes fluttered down from the sky, as soft as feathers. I shook my numb hands in an attempt to get some warmth and feeling back into them while I waited for another guide to take off with her team. As it was early in the winter, the snow had set in, but we were still getting the odd, slightly warm day, which caused a bit of a thaw. Today was not one of those days – it was absolutely freezing – but yesterday had been warm enough to cause a thaw. I marvelled at how the temperature could change so quickly as everything had frozen again overnight.

When I was able to feel my hands again, I readied my team and then took off cheering and hooting into the fresh morning air. My team charged on with excitement as we headed out into the woods.

I yelled 'Haaa!' to my team and, as my lead dogs' ears perked up in acknowledgment, we flew around to the left and onto a new trail. It wasn't long before we caught up to the other team, which had left the kennel a few minutes before us. I slowed my team down in order to keep a reasonable gap between us until I had enough space to pass them.

I knew that not far ahead on the trail I would need to halt my team to check for vehicles before crossing a road. What made this tricky in comparison to a normal halt was a swampy area stretching for about 40 metres that had a stream running down the centre of it, and we would only get back onto solid ground about 20 metres before the road. Given I was running a team of 10 dogs that was at least 10 metres long, there wasn't much room to stop the team after passing the stream and the swamp. This had been tricky in autumn but, thankfully, at this time of year with the snow set in, the swamp and the stream, which varied from being knee-deep to hip-deep, were frozen over, so we were able to run the dogs straight across the ice.

This morning though, I hadn't quite taken yesterday's thaw into account as much as I should have, and I had assumed the top layer would have frozen over again. Rushing through the woods, I watched the other guide and her team skate across the frozen stream and through the swamp area without any trouble. I was only a moment behind and was alarmed to see a strip through the middle of the frozen surface, where the previous sled had crossed, had cracked into floating ice chunks. It hadn't frozen completely like I had expected.

Crap! I was heading straight for the water at speed with no time to stop my team, none of whom were fond of going through icy water. Without skipping a beat, they charged towards the stream. For a moment, I was relieved they were going to remain on course despite the water, and I just hoped I wouldn't sink. Then, at the last second, they veered to one side and jumped for the icy edges of the broken strip, which was still frozen over and hadn't yet shattered, almost flipping my sled into the brutally cold water in the process.

As my huskies swerved onto the unbroken side of the frozen swamp, not far from the stream in the middle, they managed to stay on the slippery ice above the surface. As it turned out, sleds don't float. With the speed they managed to maintain, I was almost water-skiing as I tried to stay afloat over the cracked ice. I only just managed to stay above the surface as I held on and tried to veer over onto the hard unbroken surface too.

Amid the kerfuffle and chaos, my sled was halfway across when my lead dogs disregarded my command to turn right and instead took the drier, easier route to the left. I needed to stop them, but it wasn't easy given my snow hook punched through the surface of the ice.

I managed to lean out to the left side of my sled as we brushed past a tree frozen into the swamp and I grabbed on with all my might to halt the team. My dogs didn't want to cross the last little part of the swamp where the previous sled had broken the ice, to take the right turn, so they just stood there on the left-hand side where the ice hadn't cracked yet. It was an absolute debacle. I tied my quick release around the tree and got off my sled, then I dashed from ice chunk to ice chunk to reach the front of the team.

My lead huskies still weren't having a bar of the uninviting water to the right, so I had to physically pull them around to show them they could still make it without getting too wet. Thankfully, it worked and my lead dogs lined up in the new direction, hungry for more action, pulling against their harnesses once again.

I headed back to the sled and the second I got back, I tugged on my quick release. My team took off in the right direction and the sled dipped below the surface as it cut across the final section of the swamp. It all happened so quickly that the freezing water didn't get a chance to seep properly into my thick boots.

Once past the swampy stream and the road crossing, we were back on track. My feet were slightly damp but not fully wet, which was extremely lucky as we were at the start of an eight-hour run!

It was a wonderful but long day out in the woods, and as the sun went down that afternoon, I headed back in the direction of the kennel. The trees lost their form to the dusk shadows in the woods, so I grabbed my head torch out of my dry sack as we whisked across the snow-packed trail.

Dusk is when wolves might appear out of the woods, so I liked being able to see what was around me. This last few kilometres back to the kennel felt like a game of gladiators. With my dim head torch, I had next to no vision of oncoming obstacles that could knock me off my sled. Staying on my sled in the darkness took all my concentration; moving at high speed, I needed to duck under branches before getting clotheslined while also predicting the severity of each corner so I didn't get off balance and flip my sled.

Eventually, I made it back towards the dreaded stream crossing. I knew my dogs were well aware of the oncoming stream, this morning's chaotic crossing still fresh in their minds. I stopped well before the swampy edges so my dogs could reset and wouldn't panic as they got to the water's edge.

While we were halted in the woods, a wolf let out a howl in the distance. In the otherwise silent night, I could hear it crystal clear and my dogs could too. This was not a good sign.

OK, it was go time. I pulled my snow hook out of the ground and gave my team the command to go. They surged ahead, eager to make it back to the kennel for warm meat soup. As soon as the swampy stream was in view, my dogs bolted for the frozen side of the shattered ice strip, not wanting to go near the icy water in the middle.

I had hoped it would have frozen over during the day but, to my bitter disappointment, it had got worse. My crossing that morning must have had more of an effect on the thin ice than I realised, as the frozen ice edges had decreased dramatically in size. While the front half of the team made it onto the hard ice edge, the back half lunged for the opposite side when they could see the icy surface breaking up completely. This caused the front of the team to go for a dip. It didn't work out well having half of the team on either side of the shattered ice, all tugging in different directions. The consequence of this was my sled was directly in the middle … then they stopped.

My sled sunk in thigh-deep ice water and in I went with it. My feet had already been numb for the whole eight hours of the run after our earlier exploits at the stream, so soon I couldn't feel anything from my knees down except for the sharp stabbing of my feet freezing.

I jumped off my sunken sled and waded through the stream to the front of my team. I grabbed my lead dogs and pulled them and the rest of the team forward for about 25 metres to get them all out of the water.

Once the lead dogs made it to dry land, they were off quicker than a cat out of water, pulling the rest of the team with them. The rest of the team on the gang line were in a tangled mess, and as the team flew past me, I looked back into the darkness just in time to see my sled coming at me. As it went past, I managed to grab the handlebars and held on as tight as I could.

With a death grip on the handlebars, I was dragged along, unable to get my feet onto the sled and it was impossible to reach the snow hook to halt the team. The only way to stop now was to roll my sled and create as much resistance as I could. As I was getting dragged along, I braced myself then jolted my weight a little, flipping my sled, which wasn't hard as it was a narrow race sled.

I was now getting dragged along on my belly, digging in my feet to add more resistance, until the team finally stopped. Once stopped and with my snow hook securely jammed in the ground, I sat up. I was covered in snow and my soaked pants crackled and crunched as I moved – they had already frozen completely. I got up and had to laugh at how ridiculous this situation was as I untangled my husky team, trying to make my numb legs, which now felt like solid stumps, cooperate and keep moving.

As soon as I had the team untangled, we took off again and sped back to the kennel as fast as we could. After several long and painful minutes, we made it back. Once I'd tied up my dogs safely, I tried to sprint to the cabin but kept falling over the dead weights at the end of my legs.

Once inside, I ripped off my boots and was a little shocked by my white, waxy feet. The other guides were horrified at the sight of my dead-looking feet. Dancing around in stabbing pain as my feet thawed, I was very relieved when the first bit of colour started to come back to them. This was followed by a gradual return of feeling in them until I could wiggle my toes! The other guides laughed as I told them about my refreshing night dip. I wouldn't be taking that trail again anytime soon, that was for sure.

GIVE EVERYTHING A GO

Giving something new a go can be the special key that opens the door to leading a more fulfilling life. Being open to new experiences and saying 'yes' in the face of a challenge can help to get the most out of life. The new ventures we take on don't have to be radical. They may be as simple as taking up the hobby or sport you've always wanted to have a go at.

When we stop accepting challenges or trying new things, we stop moving forwards. Giving things a go means we give ourselves the opportunity to learn, to grow and to understand more about the world.

It's crazy what life can bring you when you are open to doing things and what, in turn, can cross your path. I have heard someone say, 'One opportunity used wisely, can change your life dramatically', which I think is very true. It doesn't matter what your opportunity relates to, whether it is work, hobbies, adventures or experiences – any opportunity can be learnt from and can lead to new endeavours in life.

Sometimes we need courage to give something outside of our comfort zone a go. We may try to give ourselves an easy out by saying things like 'the timing isn't right', but the timing may never be right. You are your own rule-maker and if you want to give it a go, why not now?

There is an old Chinese proverb: 'The best time to plant a tree was 20 years ago. The second best time is now.' I think this is a great one to remind us that it is never too late – the best time is now.

Our view is that, to progress in life, the best thing to do is to go for it and give things a go, to try, to learn, to challenge, to fail, to develop, to experience and to keep going. If you have this as your mindset, you'll be able to achieve a good number of the things you want to do in life and you'll also feel proud you've seized the opportunities that came your way.

Spending a winter dog sledding was an opportunity that I chose to take up and it has given me some priceless memories. I gained so much out of that experience and, although there were some gruelling days in sub-zero conditions, I loved every day of it.

RACING IN THE MOUNTAINS

Chapter 7

Racing in the Mountains

Oregon, USA

AMBER

The 400-mile dog sled race in Alaska that I and one of the other guides had been training our teams for was cancelled last minute due to horrendous weather conditions. After an entire season of training our race teams, we were devasted when we got the news just a few days before we were supposed to be on the road. Through some miracle, we managed to pull off altering our direction completely and, instead of heading north to Alaska, we headed west to Oregon. Before then, I had never heard of Oregon, but it was soon well on my radar after I'd learnt that the Eagle Cap Extreme Dog Sled Race was being held in the Wallowa Mountains in the north-eastern part of the state.

Competing in a 200-hundred-mile (325-kilometre) race through the mountains was going to be one hell of a challenge for me, coming from Michigan, where our dogs were trained on flat ground. Dog sled races involve strategising and some serious mushing skills. If you let them, the dogs will run their hearts out, going as hard and fast as they can and burn out rather than pacing themselves for distance. It's up to the musher to slow the team down and keep them at a pace they can maintain for the whole race. It's important for the musher to read the dogs, which comes easier when you know your huskies well, to see which ones have all the energy and which ones are tiring, and to swap positions accordingly.

One of the kennel owners helped me and the other guide load up the two 14-dog teams and all our stores into the purpose-built trailer with stacked kennels, and we headed out on the road. Our road trip took us pretty much the whole way across the United States from east to west, and we clocked up almost 3000 kilometres on the way. We rotated drivers, so we could continue driving through the night, and only stopped to let the dogs have a run around and stretch their legs, while they gobbled down some food.

In less than three days, we made it to Oregon just in time for the briefing the day before the race, which was based out of a little town called Joseph. It was a quiet, modest country town in the snowy mountains. All the shops and bars seemed to have a country cowboy theme, which gave the place an authentic Wild West feel.

The day after we arrived in Joseph was race day. I could barely sit still to eat breakfast I was so excited. It was a beautiful, sunny day and it felt good to have the weather on our side for a change. It was almost warm in Oregon, compared to what we were used to in Michigan. We were still in the snowy weather, but it was noticeably pleasant here, compared with Michigan's -40°C temperatures.

For the race, we had to carry everything we'd need for the full 325 kilometres on our little race sleds. My sled was packed tightly with food for the dogs as well as for myself, a cooker and fuel, an axe for emergencies, snowshoes and my personal gear, which included a spare pair of gloves. If I lost a glove out on the trail, it could mean the end of the race as I knew I wouldn't make it far with one hand exposed.

The race start was at a ski area on the base of a mountain just outside Joseph, and the first competitor was due to start at midday. From then onwards, the teams set off from the starting line at ten-minute intervals, one after the other. I drew bib number 10, so was tenth in the starting order. When I met the other competitors, I felt a little out of my depth to say the least. Most of them had competed here before and all of them had years of experience mushing. I was the only rookie entered, and the other mushers warned me about keeping out a keen eye for the scarce markers, as it could be easy to lose the trail.

Looking at the beginning of the course from the competitors' waiting area, I could see there was no margin for error out of the start chute. For the first couple hundred metres, there were crowds of spectators on each side of the course until the trail took a sharp 90-degree turn and headed up the first mountain. The crowd was at its thickest right by this corner, and the reason for this became obvious soon after the first competitors started. These experienced mushers were flying out of the starting chute with their over-excited dogs, then hitting the corner at full pace and absolutely stacking it in front of the spectators. If the musher was lucky, they would manage to hang onto their flipped sled and, while getting dragged along, they would right their sled and struggle away while they pulled themselves back up onto it. (The number 1 rule of dog sledding: *never* let go of your sled. Your team doesn't stop if you're not on the sled and you'll never catch them.)

When I witnessed this happen to a few very experienced mushers, it certainly got my nerves going as I realised this probably indicated I didn't have a chance. I gave myself a little pep talk: 'You've got this. You'll be fine. You've done this before. Just hit it at pace, and if you're going to go down, you'll go down in style!' I'm not sure if that last bit was the best advice to give myself.

I had my team of 12 huskies harnessed up, leaving two spare dogs with the owner. I tied each one onto the gang line in order, ready to go, then put fresh booties on all of their paws. I did my final preparations, double- and triple-checking my set up and going over each dog.

The race atmosphere was wild, and this was showing just as much in the dogs as in the people. I was bubbling with nervous energy as I jumped on my tied-off sled and watched as the ninth musher took off out of the starting chute. I was the next musher to be called up to the starting line.

A race official on a four-wheel motorbike parked next to my sled, and I tied off to it as my anchor while being escorted to the starting chute. It was all happening. I was in position at the starting line and my dogs were leaping and barking with excitement as they lunged forwards, ready to go, picking up the energy from the crowd. The countdown came over the loudspeaker: 'Three … two … one … GOOOO!'

I pulled my quick release, and we launched forwards from the starting line, taking off like bats out of a cave. Twelve of the biggest, baddest, strongest Alaskan huskies were using all their power to pull as hard as they could and within seconds we were going seriously fast. I tried with all my might to slow down my over-excited team for the fast-approaching corner, but my efforts had no effect whatsoever. As well as intensely focusing on slowing down by jamming on the brake mat with both feet, I was also trying to grab up my quick-release rope, which was dragging along on the ground beside me. I needed to get it tucked away before it snagged on something, but the corner was coming up way too quickly!

I leant out from my sled as the trailing rope bounced over the icy surface. I managed to grab it between the tips of my fingers and tuck it away just before we approached the 90-degree obstacle. In the few seconds left of lead up into the corner, I had to decide whether to brake or lean to counter the imbalance. Braking with all my weight on the rubber matt would have slowed us down a little to go around the corner, but the downside was my weight would be in the wrong place to keep the sled upright, with flipping being the likely outcome. The second option was to lean my body weight into the tight corner, so my sled would be nicely balanced. The downside of this was I couldn't brake at the same time and would be going too fast on such a tight corner, so I'd probably flip anyway. I could now see the predicament the previous mushers had been in. It seemed to be a lose–lose situation.

I made a split-second decision to go with the leaning option and, boy, did I hit that corner with some pace. The slick ice surface rushed past me in a blur as I used all my weight and might to lean into the tight corner. I was hanging off my sled with one leg cocked out sideways as I skidded the full 90 degrees around the corner like a rally car driver.

A cheer came up from the spectators as I continued up the mountain and out of view. I was as shocked as the spectators were, if not more, that I'd managed to stay on my sled! My adrenaline was pumping and I had a huge grin across my face at the fluke of having made it this far.

After the bedlam of the starting chute, I spent the next few peaceful hours heading up the twisting trail, to reach the top of the first mountain. As my team of huskies and I wound up the mountain, the sun shone brightly in the turquoise sky and the only sound was the creaking of the pines as mounds of snow fell from their branches.

At the top of the first mountain, we cruised along the ridgeline before descending the other side. Given the dogs had never trained on hills, let alone mountains, I was delighted at how much energy they had after the first big ascent. I was still having difficulty trying to keep the team at a reasonable pace, and now I was preparing for a thrilling ride down the other side. I would have to give it my undivided attention and full concentration to make it down still on my feet and in one piece.

As we started going down the mountain, I had all my weight on the brake pad to slow down the team as much as possible. Even so, we zoomed down lightning fast. My huskies were loving the rush of going down the slopes and weren't having a bar of slowing down, so we were not far off being totally out of control.

Then we started hitting switchbacks ... uh-oh! The last thing you want to do when you are cranking it down a mountain almost out of control is make a tight, 180-degree turn. Adding to this, these switchbacks had a bank on one side and a ledge that dropped off down the mountain on the other. We hurtled around the first switchback way too fast for comfort. I skidded around the whole turn with only one side of the sled in contact with the ground. I was just centimetres from skidding over the ledge and down a nasty drop. The rest of the way down went pretty much the same – over-excited dogs hitting switchbacks way too fast, resulting in several extremely close calls while I hung on by the skin on my teeth.

I breathed out with a sigh of relief when we made it to the bottom of the first mountain. I felt like I had held my breath the whole way down. I was a little surprised that we hadn't come to grief – yet. Just up ahead on the trail I could make out some sort of red structure in the distance. I noticed a red marker before the structure, which reassured me that at least I was going the right way. As we sped towards it, I realised the structure was a narrow wooden bridge. I wasn't as worried about the bridge as I was about the tight left turn I had to make to get onto the bridge and what might happen if we missed it.

I concentrated hard to judge the distances and calculate the right angle to take the corner to make it onto the bridge. As we got closer, I studied the bend, realising how you could get quite unlucky if your dogs cut the corner, which they often do. If a corner gets cut, the last thing around the corner, which is the sled, cuts it the most. And in this particular case, the dogs would make it onto the bridge but the sled would either hit the bridge railings at full pace or miss the bridge completely and go off the bank ... EEK!

As my lead dogs started getting close, I yelled 'Haaaa!' for my team to take the left turn onto the bridge. The lead dogs perked up their ears and responded accordingly, taking the team around the turn and onto the bridge – and sure enough they cut the corner slightly.

I put all my weight into keeping my sled on the trail in an attempt to counter the inward pull towards the corner. I was balancing with one leg on the sled and the other leg off the side, digging the toe of my boot into the snow as hard as I could, which acted a bit like a rudder keeping the sled in line. With one ski of my sled on the trail and the other cutting the inside corner, I managed to just make the corner, then get up onto the bridge, missing the railing by an ant's whisker. A blade of grass would not have fit between my sled and the bridge railing as we flew past. I cheered in triumph as we made it to the other side of the bridge, which got my team of huskies all pumped up again, so they took off even faster with a renewed energy. The dogs are very in tune with their musher and will, often, mimic their musher's emotions: if the musher is excited, the dogs will be too; or if the musher is feeling down or thinks the team won't finish, the dogs pick up on this and react to it.

The next few hours of the race were more of the same thing – up and down mountains, close calls, left, right and centre, white knuckles and never a dull moment. We had three checkpoints to make within the allocated timeframes to be able to continue on the trail. At each checkpoint, the race officials had set up an area for us to pull off the trail and tie off our teams. This gave the teams a small break while the mushers checked in with race officials. It also gave us a chance to attend to our dogs, check them over and put on fresh booties if they'd worn through.

The first checkpoint was around three or four hours in. There, I gave the dogs a break while I checked them over. They were still full of energy, pulling against their harnesses, wanting to continue, so it wasn't long before we took off into the woods again.

During the race, mushers were allowed to put in as much physical effort as we liked. When we wanted to give the dogs a bit of a rest, we could kick along the ground with one foot as we stood on our sleds, or we could run alongside the sled to make it lighter (never letting go of the handlebars). It was pretty hard going, to run in huge snow boots and snow gear, so most mushers don't bother. I gave it a good go though as it also helped me to keep warm and alert.

Now that the dogs were going at a steady pace, I would hold onto the sled rail and step off the sled and run. I would sprint my heart out, until I couldn't keep the pace, then I'd quickly jump back on the sled to avoid being left behind. It was just like jumping onto a moving treadmill; after sprinting as fast as possible with the assistance of the sled handlebars pulling me through the air, I would have to make it back onto the sled before falling over when it got too fast. This only worked when we were heading up mountains as the dogs were still much too fast on flat or downhill terrain for me to keep up with them.

The day flew by as I rode through the mountains, and pretty soon the sun began to sink lower in the sky as the cool night air set in. I could sense the energy shift in dogs now, so I settled them down into a smooth endurance pace that they could comfortably sustain.

I made it to the second checkpoint a few hours after dark and, like most of the other teams, I decided to camp up for the rest of the night. Exhausted from the day's efforts, I was keen for a sit down and some food, but the dogs were my priority. I set up sleeping possies for each of my 12 huskies. There was a big pile of straw we could use, so I grabbed a bundle and made cosy straw nests on the snow for each dog so they could curl up and get some rest. I also got a little fire going and heated up a meal for the dogs, which consisted of meat chunks and high-calorie dog biscuits mixed with hot water to make a warm soup. After feeding the dogs, it was onto massaging any tight muscles they had and getting the vets to check them over if need be.

As midnight approached, I was nearly asleep on my feet. I spent a few minutes cooking up my own dinner and had a hot brew.

The dogs where long since out to it, sound asleep, twitching with the occasional woof as they dreamt of running. I had about four hours to get some shut-eye myself. I had set up camp under a tree at this checkpoint, which would offer a little shelter if the weather were to turn. Luck was on my side with kind weather – it was a beautiful, clear night. The stars were bright in the dark midnight sky and there was no wind at all.

I grabbed my sleeping bag and some warmer clothes from my sled and went to make my own little straw nest on the snow to sleep on. Unfortunately, there wasn't any straw left over for me, so it was going to be a long night. I was too exhausted to put any effort into anything else, so I jumped in my sleeping bag and lay down on the bare snow. I shivered away, as the snow sucked away any warmth I could gather. It was literally like trying to sleep in a freezer. Unsurprisingly, I didn't sleep a wink.

I didn't find it hard to get up a few hours later as I was already lying awake with my teeth chattering away. I felt like I'd been hit by a train, but at least moving around gave me some relief from the cold. I cooked up a quick breakfast and a brew – just the smell of hot coffee put a smile across my face. That hot brew was the magic that brought warmth and energy back to my body after the harsh night. It was all I needed to help me wake up and to make me feel enlivened again. There is nothing quite like having a nice hot cuppa when you are out roughing it in nature.

We headed off on the trail before dawn broke and, as soon as the sun started to come up, the scene was like something on a postcard – it was spectacular. Standing on my sled in the mountains, behind my team of huskies, the pink sky turned a fierce orange as the sun broke through the clouds. I could barely take it all in. To be here, to be able to do something so unique, so crazy, so fun, this was what life was all about.

Even after a groggy start, it was one hell of a good day's racing through the woods in the beautiful sunshine, with the snow making everything seem magical. The day flew by, and by the time the afternoon sun began to fade, we had covered a fair few miles. I knew we were nearing the last leg of the race. By this time, I was really starting to feel the effects of having no sleep the previous night, as well as the physical impact of having been on my feet mushing for the last two days straight. My eyelids were heavy and the fatigue I felt began to test my endurance.

Even though I was feeling the full effects, the dogs were still happily continuing at their steady pace, though my huskie team was now a little smaller. In this race, each team started with 12 dogs, but if any of the dogs gets hurt or isn't looking their best, you 'drop' them, or remove them from your team, so they don't have to continue any further.

If you're at a checkpoint when you need to drop a dog, you leave the dog with the vets, who will look after them and take them back to the finish line. If you are out on the trail when you need to drop a dog, you put them in your sled until you get to the next checkpoint. This might sound easy, but it can be a real drama.

My youngest dog, Charming, was the first to alter his gait by developing a very subtle limp in the early morning, so I took him off the team and put him in my sled. To make room for him, I had to rearrange all my tightly packed gear – some of it ended up dangling on the outside of my sled. Gear dangling on the outside can make a sled quite unbalanced, particularly narrow race sleds, but there's no other way to fit your gear as well as a dog inside the sled.

My sled had a material cover over it that closed with Velcro. It was pretty hard to put a dog inside it as the dog will try to jump out when you give the command to the rest of the team to take off. Thankfully, Charming was a dream to have in my sled. He curled up in a ball and went to sleep until the next checkpoint, which almost never happens.

As it got late into the second afternoon, Snoopy was my next team member to slow down. His altered gait told me that he'd either strained something or he was fatigued. Unfortunately, Snoopy was not easy like Charming had been. I had to wrestle with Snoopy to get him into the sled, then wrestle with him again to keep him in the sled. I needed more hands!

I held Snoopy, with a strained effort, in my sled while crouching down to pull my snow hook, to get the team going again. To make things just a little harder when I gave the command 'Ready … Let's go!', Snoopy thought the command was for him, so he got all excited and, despite my best endeavours, would jump out of the sled to join the team.

I had a few false starts as I struggled to catch Snoopy each time he jumped out of my sled. On what was probably my fourth attempt, we were finally away. When Snoopy finally settled, he sat in my sled for the rest of the leg (almost

70 kilometres) with just his head sticking out of the cover, looking up at me with a happy grin across his face.

Once darkness set in, I put on my head torch so I could make out the trail in front of us. The head torch was just for me, as the dogs had excellent night vision. Back in Michigan, if I was out in the woods running the dogs in the dark, I didn't bother with a head torch by the end of the season, as I knew the trails well enough to make it back to the kennel in the darkness. Although, rushing through the woods, wondering how many creatures are watching you can be quite an eerie experience, especially as I'd been stalked by a wolf more than once.

Out here, though, I wasn't familiar with the trail, so there was no way I could carry on without a head torch. If I'd tried to, I probably would have ended up in the middle of nowhere having taken a random turn on the trail, or else I might have been knocked off my sled by a rogue low-hanging tree branch, leaving the team to carry on without me.

It was nearing midnight on the second night of the race, and as crisp air brushed past me, once again the thought popped into my head, 'How grand life can be!' I reflected how lucky I was to be here. It sure wouldn't be everyone's cup of tea — it was the middle of the night, I was cold and exhausted and racing a team of huskies through snowy mountains in Oregon. But this was my cup of tea and I had chased this opportunity and consistently worked hard for it, which made this moment almost overwhelming. I reflected on how I came to be in this position — a mixture of passion for adventure, making the most of an opportunity, persistence, consistent hard yakka and seeking out opportunities. I made a mental note on the mountainside that night that this was living the spirit of adventure and one to remember.

As we pushed on through the darkness, the mental and physical exhaustion began to hit me like a tonne of bricks. I checked my watch – it was nearing 2 am. No wonder the exhaustion was catching up with me; we were 38 hours into the race by now. I hadn't slept in almost two days, my body was aching from being on my feet and my mind was drained from the constant concentration it took to guide my team of huskies.

Then to mix things up, I was hit with a nasty surprise when my head torch went out with no warning. I was startled by the suddenness of finding myself racing along in complete darkness. I was riding through the night blind, as there was no moon at all that night. I had made sure there were fresh batteries in my head torch, so it should have lasted the whole night. I got a fright as a thought flashed through my mind that the team could run off a cliff and I would have no idea. I immediately stopped the team and, to my despair, the head torch was stone-cold dead, not a wink of light left in it.

I had a backup head torch for just such an occasion. Once I'd pulled it out and flicked it on, I got the team going again. I was a little nervous now, as this torch was nowhere near as bright as the first one and, worst of all, now I had no back-up if this torch decided to give up on me.

The dogs continued full pace in the darkness while I struggled to see in the dim light of my head torch. I was only just making out the trail in time to make the turns to keep the team going in the right direction.

I was sure the finish line was close, perhaps an hour away, so I prayed that my second head torch would last that long. Batteries can lose their charge if they get too cold and I had a suspicion this torch wasn't the best in the first place, as I had limited resources in Michigan. Then, out of nowhere, this second head torch flicked off. Noooooo! Before I could stop the team, it flicked back on again. I was really dancing with the devil now. I knew that this flicking on and off was what this torch did to warn you the battery was low – oh crap, that finish line had better be close!

While on one hand I was fretting about the torch, on the other hand I was just about falling asleep on my feet – literally. My eyelids felt almost too heavy to stay open and I blinked in slow motion to get the slightest relief. I was fighting as hard as I could to push through the exhaustion. I tried everything from running next to the sled to grabbing handfuls of snow off the trail and rubbing them on my forehead just to keep myself awake.

As we rushed through the darkness on the narrow trail, at times I would start to nod off and almost fall off my sled. At one point, I dozed off while I was standing on my sled and my legs buckled underneath me. I woke with a sharp pain and the sound of a crack as my chin hit the sled's handlebars. That woke me up! Luckily, my hands hadn't let go of the sled when my legs had given out. I'm not sure how I managed it, but I was still on the sled, thank goodness.

Soon, the dim light of my torch hit a reflective sign. It was the welcoming sight I'd been waiting for. It confirmed that I was only half an hour from the finish line. This gave me a prickle of energy that was enough to push me to stay awake until the end.

By this stage of the race, I was down to eight dogs out of my team of 12. After I'd left Charming and Snoopy at checkpoints, I had taken two of my other dogs off the team and they were both in my sled with me now.

Having two dogs in my sled meant it was a whole new level of unbalanced, as all my gear was hanging on the outside so they could fit under the cover. To make things worse, these two dogs both liked to know what was going on, so they moved around constantly, popping their heads out of the cover and shifting their body weight as we went, which I would have to counter continuously to keep us upright.

The final kilometre of the race may have been the most extreme and most exciting part of the whole race. It was all downhill – and not just downhill but a steep downhill with banks on either side. With my sled constantly on the verge of flipping, I gripped on tightly with white knuckles. Added to that, I had two dogs in my off-balance sled and there were also plenty of sharp corners and lots of trees to hit. Great.

After all of this, I was sure as hell going to finish this race, so down the mountain I went. I was braking with all my strength, putting my weight on the rubber mat while also using all my weight to counter the sloping ground to keep the sled upright and on the trail. At the same time, I kept hold of the two dogs in the sled with one hand, to stop them from jumping out to run amid the chaos.

Through sheer luck, I managed to hold everything together – just! We sped down the trail in the pitch-black woods lit only by my faint head torch. The woods were a blur of dark shadows as we flashed past; by the time I managed to make out a tree branch and register what it was, I would have half a second to duck under it. Several times I thought my sled was going to flip over, but I kept reminding myself that flipping was not an option, as I was so close to the finish now.

At one point, we came over a small knob and started to drop down a steep part of the trail. I couldn't see more than 40 metres in front of me, but I could just make out the bulk of something big up ahead. I was puzzled. It was something unusually large to be in the woods and man-made blocking the trail. I strained, putting the last of my energy on the brake, frantically trying to work out what the structure was as we rushed towards it.

My lead dogs were no more than 20 metres away from it when I realised that it was a wall of bloody hay bales! What on earth was a wall of hay bales doing blocking the trail?

The bales were neatly stacked, one on top of the other, at least six high, and there was no way around the wall as there were trees on either side of it. I was only a few seconds away from it and I was still stumped, but I didn't have the luxury of time to figure it out.

Half a second later, I clicked when I made out some tracks going around it to the right – it was a 90-degree turn. 'GEEEEE!' I yelled out to my team and my lead huskies took my team swiftly round to the right with less than 10 metres to spare.

It was a tight corner and I had called it much too late. My team made it around the turn with no trouble but, as I skidded after them, my sled went out wide. I skidded and hit the hay bales side-on. While my shoulder felt the impact, it was my sled that bore the brunt of the blow. The dog team, however, didn't stop so I was soon being pulled forwards as my team continued on the trail. I looked back at the hay bale wall and could see where the snow was all kicked up around it. It appeared some other teams hadn't made the turn in time either.

Throughout this last kilometre of trail, I had a constant stream of adrenaline pumping through me, and the dogs were thriving with the thrill of the terrain. The trail was testing me with each new descent feeling steeper than the last. When I looked up and saw pure darkness as my dogs disappeared downwards two at a time, I thought we had gone off a ledge. As the sled went over after them, I realised it wasn't a ledge, but the trail was simply that steep. It was a bit like being on a roller coaster, except you could hit trees and fall off at any point.

Before I knew it, the ground had flattened out and we were at the bottom of the slope. Suddenly, I saw a dull glow, then lights ahead – the finish line!

I crossed the finish line in one piece, with my dogs in good shape, a bit after 3 am. What a journey! I'd covered 325 kilometres in 39.45 hours, including breaks. I felt overwhelmed by having finished the race. I knew I was at the back end of the field, but I didn't care. My dogs had been outstanding, considering they had only trained on flat ground and weren't used to the terrain.

I let the two dogs out of the sled, and they jumped around happily, wagging their tails and trying to get all the attention. I gave every dog a heap of belly rubs and a good old scratch, which they lapped up. Then I gave them a huge helping of warm meat soup, which they gobbled up enthusiastically.

We made our way back to the accommodation, where I relaxed in the hot shower before bed. Hot water had never felt so good. After some good tucker, I was out cold in a deep, over-exhausted sleep with a grin on my face.

SEEK OUT OPPORTUNITY

To seek out an opportunity is to create momentum in the direction you want to head in. It's not just about taking the opportunities that come your way, but also about doing things to create those opportunities. You can't just wait around for things to happen; instead, you need to get out there and apply yourself to *make* things happen. And, even then, if opportunity doesn't knock, you might have to beat on that door with a bit of determination until it presents itself.

By creating and pursuing opportunities, we allow ourselves to have new experiences, to grow as people, to gain perspective and to create memories to treasure.

Not all these experiences or memories are going to be good, so remember that it takes bad experiences to make you realise just how amazing the good ones are. I reckon we probably learn equally from both the good and the bad, as the failures we experience can teach us a great deal while also helping to prepare us for success.

The more perspective we gain and the more we learn from giving things a go, the more we can apply this to other parts of our lives to help us with further opportunities. I like the saying, 'The pessimist sees difficulty in every opportunity, while the optimist sees opportunity in every difficulty.' Opportunities sure can be what the beholder makes them.

Whether the opportunity you seek out is big or small, physical or mental, professional or personal, it is normal for it to make you feel nervous. We don't need to focus on thinking there should be no fear, but, rather, we should focus on channelling this fear into excitement, which will then help us to take the leap into the unknown.

Often, you'll have to push yourself out of your comfort zone in order to create opportunities. You have to try new things, meet new people and explore new places in order to gain life experience and understanding. Every accomplishment starts with an opportunity that has been seized or created, and then the decision behind it to give it a go, to try.

SAILING ACROSS THE PACIFIC

Chapter 8

Sailing Across the Pacific

Hawai'i to San Francisco

AMBER

Through a series of wild, crazy, fun adventures in numerous countries, I found myself living in Hawai'i and working as a divemaster, taking tourists out on scuba dive charters in warm, tropical waters every day.

After an extremely cold winter dog sledding and an even colder time mountaineering in Alaska with Serena, we both wanted to go somewhere warm, so we headed to Hawai'i.

Taking people diving in Hawai'i was more than a dream job for me — it was a far-fetched, too-good-to-be-true, dream job. Even so, I backed myself as I had been scuba diving for as long as I could remember. Why couldn't I do it?

After researching and applying for several dive positions, I was stoked when I landed a job. I'd loosely planned to spend a dive season working in Hawai'i, and time really flew by. Most days, I would take two charters out diving, and I probably had as much fun as my clients.

Out on a dive charter one day, one of the clients was a very entertaining older chap, who clearly loved a good yarn. He had well-leathered skin and pale, glassy, sun-damaged eyes, which were clearly the result of a lifetime spent in the harsh sun.

He soon started to tell us about his sailing adventures all over the world. His yarns planted the seed in my head of doing a sailing voyage. It was something fresh and exciting that I hadn't tried before and the chase of a new adventure was just too tempting. I decided right then and there I would have one last epic adventure to finish off my travels, by sailing home to New Zealand.

My plan was to find a small sailing boat that I could crew on. I was after a proper, legit sailing experience, not a blasé cruise boat ride, so I put up posters at the local yacht club in Waikiki and signed up to numerous websites to find a boat to join. This was certainly one of those times when I had to seek out the opportunity and make it happen for myself.

While I was on the hunt for a crewing spot to sail back to New Zealand, I met a lovely young fella on one of my dive charters. He told some fantastic stories about working at remote sites in Bolivia, where he'd spent time walking jaguars and pumas on a leash through the Amazon jungle.

'What? You said walking jaguars ... and pumas? In the

Amazon?' I asked, barely believing what I was hearing. After all, in my job, I'd got pretty used to tourists with their tall tales and took most of them with a grain of salt. I thought this fella's story must have included a hell of a lot of exaggeration, but I figured that if even half of it was true, it would be an adventure worth having.

That evening, I looked up the place he'd been talking about, and I nearly fell off my chair when I realised the whole story had been true! A new seed had been planted, and there was no way I could sail home to New Zealand now, not a chance. However, sailing was still on the agenda — it was just going to be in the other direction, back towards the US mainland, so I could easily fly on to Bolivia.

As fate would have it, the very next day I received a response to one of my many applications, which was from a guy who needed a crew to sail a boat from Hawai'i to San Francisco. Boom, perfect!

I went to meet the boat's captain at the marina to interview for the position. I had spent the hour before the interview googling sailing lingo and YouTubing how to sail. In the interview, I threw around a few sailing terms, sounding like I knew what I was doing and only alluded to my minimal sailing experience. Even 'minimal' *might* have been slightly exaggerated as I had almost zero sailing experience, except for having tried sailing in a very basic one-person sailboat when I was a young child. I was stoked when given a crew position on the spot and it was all go as we were leaving in less than a week.

I spent the next few days scrambling around, getting organised. I sold my beautiful pink moped, said goodbye to the crew at my local CrossFit gym and hung out with my mates for the last time. My dive bosses, an awesome American couple, took my resigning at short notice surprisingly well, possibly because they had been impressed by some of my adventures and, with the dive season coming to an end, they had known it was only a matter of time before I hit the next one. They were almost as excited by my next adventure as I was and even took me out for a farewell dinner at the best restaurant on the island!

The sailing boat for our journey was a 48-foot Tayana, which was small for the big, wide ocean but luxurious for a small sailing boat. The point of the trip was to deliver the boat to its owners in San Francisco. They wanted their boat sailed across the Pacific Ocean to mainland America but were too old to make the voyage themselves.

As well as the captain and me, there were another three crew members on the voyage. Our departure got delayed by a few days as a result of hurricanes off the coast of Hawai'i. Once the weather settled, we eventually set sail at midday on Friday, 14 August 2015.

I was 24 years old at the time and, with basically zero sailing experience, I was the least experienced out of everyone, although I didn't exactly advertise this. The other crew members were a similar age to me, so we all got on pretty well. Juliana was a hippy girl, who had sailed only a few times before. I ended up getting on well with her and we hung out together a bit once we got to San Francisco. Then there was Melinda, who had a fair amount of experience and dreamed of sailing around the world. She was loud and pretty entertaining, always chattering away, but it got a little too much at times while we were confined to a small space in the middle of the ocean. The final crew member was Ryan, who had a lot of experience. He owned his own sailboat in Canada and wouldn't leave the ocean unless he had to. He was an interesting character, with many stories of roughing it with no money, trying to busk his way through countries and getting out of a few crazy situations, the sort they make horror movies about.

Brian, the captain, was in his late thirties, and we also got on well. He had pretty much lived his whole life on boats, as his parents were sailors. In 1996, he briefly held the world record as the youngest person to do a solo circumnavigation of the world. As well as being a great person to learn from, he was also very chilled out and funny, for which I was extremely thankful as I'd heard some terrible stories of voyages with impossible captains.

The voyage was around 4250 kilometres as the crow flies, but, of course, we weren't crows and we wouldn't be going in a straight line, so we would cover a fair few more kilometres than that by tacking back and forth. It was estimated that we'd take about 17 days (maybe only 14 if the weather was good) to get to San Francisco. As it turned out, because of the weather conditions en route, we covered a gruelling 5600 kilometres during our trip, which took 25 days to complete. The captain had done this trip 32 times, and said he'd never once had such peculiar weather or taken so long. He thought it was due to global warming.

I will never forget that first night out on the ocean – the absolute torture of it! It had started out calm in the afternoon, and we were all quick to celebrate our departure with a beer or two. By the evening, we had left Oahu behind and, with it, the calm water.

Out in the rough open seas, Juliana was the first one to feel the urge to purge due to the motion of the ocean. The waves had a sharp chop to them that seemed to slap our little sailing boat around, but I was pleasantly surprised that I still felt fine. A few hours later, though, it was a totally different story. By nightfall, both Juliana and I were making regular trips to the side of the boat to feed the fish.

In the past, I'd suffered from a bit of seasickness, but during the months I'd spent working on the dive boat I hadn't been seasick once (although that might have been because I was diving so much). I was so damned confident that I wouldn't get seasick on this sailing voyage that I hadn't even considered bringing seasickness tablets.

As the boat crashed through huge waves, it repeatedly heeled over, with one side touching the water's surface while the other side was up in the air. We were getting tossed from side to side with the mast almost skimming the water on the port side as the boat rolled over the waves. Meanwhile, every few minutes, waves crashed over the boat, attempting to wash overboard anything that wasn't tied down.

Too sick to be concerned, Juliana and I clung to the port-side railings for dear life. We wore harnesses that were tied off to the centre pole so we couldn't get washed overboard, but we were being dipped into the raging ocean each time the boat rolled from side to side.

Throughout the night, we squatted there, clinging to the hand rail, soaked to the bone, and routinely spewed over the side while giant waves crashed over our heads, forcing saltwater into our eyes, ears and mouths. With weak, shaking knees and trembling hands, we would crawl like spiders through the night to wrestle our way back up onto the bench seats in the middle of the boat. Still in a singlet and shorts from the earlier heat of day, but now shivering profusely (which was the least of our worries, given how sick we felt), we would pass out there for half an hour before we would wake to begin the routine again. This lasted until 5.30 am and it felt like it had been the longest night ever. I never spewed again after the first night (probably because I had no food left in me); however, I felt pretty rotten for the first three days and very average for the four after that.

For the next seven days, the weather did not let up, not even briefly. These extremely rough seas were the result of the hurricanes that had delayed our departure. We later found out that three more of them had hit while we were battling those hectic seas. No wonder we were surfing rollers!

For the first week, we headed directly north and even slightly west at times. We did this until we hit the weather high or the trade winds, which would allow us to head east towards the mainland. We averaged 240 to 270 kilometres a day, which was great headway.

Despite making good progress, we had a few dramas in that first week. On Day 3, the generator gave up, and on Day 4 the alternator on the engine gave out, so we had no way to charge batteries and no power. As a result, we scoffed down as much of our fresh food out of the fridge as we could before it went off. This meant gorging on huge meals of fresh food that was meant to last most of the trip. We had no choice, though, as it would all spoil in the heat without refrigeration. On Day 6, we got the alternator going, but by that time all the fresh food was pretty much devoured, and we only had canned food for the rest of the trip – bugger!

Amid all the gear failures, a call came in on the satellite phone. It was from a friend of the captain's, who was crying hysterically and asking if we were OK. We were a little confused. She explained that the US Coast Guard were making their final preparations and fuelling up a plane to head out looking for us because we'd set off our emergency position indicating radio beacon (EPIRB) less than an hour before.

Still confused, we opened our ditch bag and sure enough, our EPIRB was going off. This was clearly the result of a malfunction, as the tab hadn't been pulled. Having assured Brian's friend we were fine, a hasty call was made to the Coast Guard to let them know what had happened and to assure them we didn't need rescuing. Meanwhile, a canister on one of the life jackets attached to a harness self-fired, inflating the jacket to be ready for an emergency – weird. Sailors can be a superstitious bunch and the captain wondered if there was a deeper meaning or perhaps even a warning behind this odd chain of events.

During that first week, we hit a lot of squalls. Until then, I had no idea what a squall was. Crap! That was something I'd missed when learning the sailing lingo on YouTube. I learnt pretty quickly though. We were cruising along and I was looking out towards the horizon when I saw a hazy patch of water with mist above it. That hazy patch of water almost had a living quality about it as the mist mysteriously crept across the water until it reached us.

As we sailed into the mist, it was like stepping through a door into a storm. Instantly, the wind went crazy, the sea did its best to capsize us and heavy rain pelted down. In the squall, we were tossed around like a toy boat in the big, wide ocean, then, about an hour later, we got spat out the other side into the normal day's weather.

The worst squall hit us at about 1 am on the fifth night, and it was like nothing I had ever experienced before. Mother Nature was clearly putting us through her fiercest test. Ryan was on watch at the time, and he came stumbling down the stairs into the cabin and woke us all up. The squall had hit so quickly that Ryan hadn't had time to wake us, and now the boat was suddenly getting thrown violently from side to side. Ryan had feared that the waves could sink us and wanted to make sure we were all alert and ready.

We all braced ourselves as best as we could, but, even then, it was difficult not to get slammed into the cabin walls. I peeked up through the hatch to see a scene straight out of a movie, like *The Perfect Storm* or something. Where the night sky should have been, instead of stars, I saw huge rollers coming in. These enormous waves towered over us. They were so big they totally blocked out everything else, replacing it with fierce, white wash. Our puny sailing boat didn't stand a chance of outrunning these monsters, so we had no choice but to go with them. Not wanting to be trapped in the cabin if we capsized, we all came up to the centre benches on the deck and held on to whatever we could. Each time a wave rolled by, the ocean seemed to rise and fall the height of a five-storey building.

As each wave aggressively gathered behind us, we would rise up out of the ocean as we got caught in the whitewash, then we found ourselves looking down at the enormous drop-off in front of us. We all held on as tightly as we could because there had been no time to get the harnesses on. All our eyeballs were nearly popping out of our head as terror and adrenaline took over.

Being trapped in whitewash was like being in a washing machine – it was trying to throw our tiny boat every which way. We fought to keep the boat pointing with the wave direction, then we would surf out of control down the huge waves. Many times, I thought the boat's nose was going to dig into the bottom of the wave and toss the whole boat head over keel, sending us all to Davy Jones's Locker. Later, I found out that this had been a very real possibility.

Brian was very calm, which was the only reassuring thing. He made it seem like this was an everyday occurrence for him and told us just to ride it out. Later, he did admit that this was right up there with the worst storm he had seen.

Eventually, the storm subsided as quickly as it had come on, but tension and excitement still hung in the air. Now that it was over, I had a good chuckle in the darkness of the night at what I'd just experienced. I'd hoped for a moment exactly like this; not the dangerous, nearly sinking part but more the being thrown around in a giant storm. I just wanted to know what it was like.

During our second week at sea, the weather calmed down, and the boat was almost level for a whole day. I saw plenty of wildlife along the way – many dolphins, whales and seals and there was even a friendly neighbourhood albatross that followed us for two weeks straight. We had many beautiful sunsets and stunning sunrises. The nights were also beautiful when phosphorescent plankton would light up the ocean like a million fairy lights and the twinkling stars would light up the sky, creating a tranquil, almost surreal scene.

It's in the moments like this, when I take a minute to reflect on things, that I truly grasp what is important in life. I'm not a particularly spiritual person, but nature has a way of clearing my head and allowing me to think about the important things. Often, when you take that extra moment to stare at a beautiful sunset, to look up and take in the starry night sky, or to get up early to watch the sky change colours, that's when you realise all the little things that are easy to get caught up in and worry about that aren't that important at all.

With the weather having calmed down, it was almost smooth sailing for a while, and we even got some fishing in. Using a hand line, I hooked up a lure and threw the line in. Within half an hour, I had us a beautiful mahi-mahi.

I'd done a fair bit of fishing back home, and this was like hitting the jackpot. The fish was just over 1 metre long, and it meant we would finally have some fresh food again! I was a bit bemused when the other crew members said they didn't want me to kill the fish, even though they had been keen to do some fishing. We'd been eating canned slosh that barely represented food and they had wanted fresh fish for dinner but did not want to kill a fish in the process.

As the huge fish jumped and slapped around the deck, we ended up using an old technique to keep people happy – we poured rum onto the fish's gills. It immediately stopped flapping and 'went to sleep'. Not only did it calm the fish, but it also made it even tastier to eat – and it was one hell of a delicious feed for dinner!

On Day 11, we finally caught the trade winds and turned east towards San Francisco. Ye-ah! We should have hit the trade winds around Day 5, but we'd had to travel a lot further north than usual because of the weather. In fact, we were so far north that we were only about five days off hitting Alaska.

We were still another 10 to 15 days from San Francisco, which was a little demoralising for me as I was well over canned food and was becoming a bit stir crazy being confined to such a small space. I couldn't handle doing nothing every day, and after the novelty wore off, it started to become hard to deal with. I don't think I have ever sat/slept/lay down for so long in one go in my life!

Before I came on board, I was told there would be a lot of sitting around, but I didn't quite realise the extent of it, and I certainly hadn't anticipated the trip taking us nearly four weeks instead of the usual two. I had pictured doing a few workouts down the back of the boat and climbing the mast and things like that – what a joke! With the boat that heeled over and getting thrown around so much during that first week, I was lucky to take a few steps in a day let alone do a workout.

On Day 13, our autopilot broke, which made things interesting. Up until that point, the boat had pretty much steered itself, and we rotated being on watch in two-hour shifts. When we were on watch, we'd look out for other boats, large container ships when we got into the shipping lanes and rubbish that could cause us damage if we hit into it or ran it over, like big fishing nets that could get stuck on the rudder.

With the autopilot not working, we had to take a lot more notice of the compass to make sure we were steering in the right direction. This was easy enough to do and having a task that required my full attention helped make the days go by a bit quicker. For some reason, Juliana and Melinda had a lot of difficulty keeping the boat on track, so they would stare at the compass almost without blinking to keep us on track, and even then they would nearly tack us off in the other direction. Melinda was flabbergasted when she watched me staring out at the horizon and not looking at the compass when I was on watch.

In an effort to not go mad in the head from staring at a speck on the dash, I decided to use the angle of the sunlight or moonlight hitting the water to keep direction instead of the compass, which was a lot more natural. Mostly, though, I just felt the way the boat moved. Sometimes, it would move up to 60 degrees without the steering wheel moving, but I could feel the boat swinging around and quickly countered it before it took place.

I had a good chuckle when I heard the others talking about me, saying, 'She's obviously done a lot more sailing than she lets on.' I'd told them all I'd done minimal sailing and was a little vague on the details. They thought I was being modest about the 'minimal' part!

The third week was pretty uneventful. The weather finally changed from the tropical warmth to cold and cloudy, which usually happens just three days out from Hawai'i. The others could hardly believe how strange this was – in all the time they had spent on the water, they hadn't seen such peculiar weather.

By Day 16, we were in the shipping lanes and passing big container ships. For the previous two weeks, we hadn't seen a single other boat. Now, they seemed to sneak up on us all the time. It's hard to believe that out of the whole, wide ocean, it would be possible to end up in the direct path of another boat, but it turns out that's not uncommon.

One night when I was on watch, I could see the port and starboard lights of a boat in the distance. It was a pitch-black night with barely any moonlight, so I couldn't make out the size or shape of the other vessel, and without any reference points in the darkness to judge distances, it was difficult to tell the direction and speed it was going.

I woke the captain and, when I next looked up, I was shocked to see that the lights had gone from being distant dots to now towering above us only a few hundred metres away. It was something big and it was moving straight towards us at pace!

We quickly changed course and, with a few nervous glances back and forth, desperately got out of the way of what turned out to be a huge container ship. It was like three high-rise buildings on the water moving silently across the surface like a ghost through the night. It totally dwarfed us, and we probably weren't even a speck on its radar.

I've heard all sorts of stories about container ships not seeing little sailing boats and obliterating them without even knowing. The container ships would then turn up at a dock with the remnants of a sailing boat still dragging on its bow and only then realise they had hit some poor bugger.

One of the questions people always ask me is, 'How did you go to the toilet?' Well, we had two heads (toilets) down in the cabin, but I wasn't fond of cramming myself into a tiny, dark room that didn't smell the freshest. In rough seas, the confined space made me feel queasy with seasickness, and it wasn't always easy to sit there when getting thrown from side to side.

The only other option was to perch off the swim step or duckboard on the back of the boat to do your business. That was my preference — at least I could keep an eye on the horizon, which helped steady the seasickness, and I had a face full of fresh air and an ocean view (even if it was accompanied by a spray of sea salt).

In order to do that, each time I went I had to put a harness on first. Without the harness, if I slipped/fell/got washed over the side by a wave, I would likely be a goner. The boat would carry on until someone realised we were a person down, and the likelihood of finding someone in the open water was extremely slim.

Once I had my harness on and was clipped in, I would steady myself and crawl/walk to the back of the boat as it rocked over the waves. After opening the gate on the hand railing, I would climb down the ladder (out of view of the rest of the boat) and onto the swim step.

The swim step was level with the water, so my feet would get a refreshing dip each time, and I'd clip my harness onto the lower rail. Harnessed up and balancing on the swim step, it was then a matter of timing things in between the waves that washed over the swim step as the ocean continuously rolled. While clinging onto the ladder to stay aboard, I had to quickly squat while hanging over the edge of the step to do my business while keeping a close eye on the next wave coming in. If that wasn't difficult enough, on the rough days, the waves would wash over me and each swell would threaten to throw me overboard, if I wasn't holding onto the ladder tightly enough.

When the bigger waves crashed over the back of the boat, it was normal for one of the crew members to pop their head over the back to make sure whoever was going to toilet was still there and that they were not getting dragged through the water by their harness, as it seemed impossible that anyone could still be clinging on, pants around their ankles, pinching a loaf before the next wave hit!

Every time you went to the toilet, it was like taking part in an extreme sport. It really kept me on my toes and alert at all times. It could be rather entertaining and I much preferred the adventure of it over using the dingy toilet onboard.

*

Right when I started to feel like there would be no end to this sea voyage, on the twenty-fourth day, we spotted land. Boy, it was good to see dry land! We were so excited we could hardly contain ourselves. Just the smell of dry land was enough to get us jumping up and down.

As we got closer, I could make out the details of San Francisco. We cracked a bottle of champagne in celebration as I steered us in under the Golden Gate Bridge and we marvelled at the city as we headed in to the marina. The boat's owners, having done a lot of sailing in their heyday, knew what it felt like to have spent so long at sea and, as we pulled up to the dock, they were there waiting for us with burgers and chips and a whole heap of fresh food!

The smell of real food after that length of time without it was phenomenal. We devoured the burgers then headed straight for the showers to scrub off more than three weeks' worth of salt. Yes, this voyage involved more than three weeks without a freshwater shower, and for all that time salt was building up in my hair, knotting it into a birds' nest.

Looking back, I'm stoked I took this voyage, even if I did get bored shitless at times, not to mention having endured the worst seasickness of my life. If I were to do another sailing trip, next time I would do one that stops at lots of different islands so I could explore places and try new things rather than spend a whole lot of time out in the big, wide ocean. But that's the thing about life, you have to experience these things to know if you will like them or not, and how much enjoyment you'll get out of them.

CONQUERING WORK-LIFE BALANCE

A work-life balance can be a difficult thing to achieve and, even when you do, it will always be something that is a work in progress. Overall, there is no right or wrong way to do it, as everyone is different. Each person enjoys different things and has different priorities in life, so this balancing act will be unique for everyone. The most important thing is to assess what makes you happy and to do more of those things, to create the balance that works for you then to strive to retain it.

Some people absolutely love their work. It gives them motivation and purpose to keep pushing on and striving higher - and that's fantastic! For others, motivation and purpose may come from things outside of work, and your job may simply be the means to fund the things you love to do. It's totally fine if you don't love your job, as long as you can still achieve a balanced lifestyle and make time for the things you do love. After all, the cold, hard reality of the world we live in is that you need money to do most things.

There is a lot of motivational content out there that tells us we all need to love what we do for work. Don't get me wrong, if you are someone who loves what you do, that is a wonderful thing and you should keep hold of it with both hands! That said, don't think there is something wrong if you don't love your job - this is OK too! There is certainly nothing wrong with your work being a way to fund the things you love. I'm not suggesting you should stay in a job you hate. There is a big difference between not loving your job versus hating it - and you should never settle for something that makes you miserable.

Whichever one of these is you, it doesn't matter, as long as you have found or are finding what works for you and it enables you to live a fulfilling life. Take a minute to assess your lifestyle: are you living it how you want to? Or have you given into the stress of what you 'think' you should be doing? For your own mental and physical wellbeing, find the things that give you purpose and make you happy.

Serena and I have always been very driven in our careers, as we have a hunger to achieve. We also have a great passion for adventure and experiencing as much as we can outside of work. Our passion for adventures has increased our drive to work hard because adventures can be expensive and we've had to work hard to be able to fund them.

Establishing a work–life balance has been extremely important to us and has enabled us to get the best out of both our work and our life outside of work. By continually assessing this balance, we are able to recognise when the scales begin to tip and things start to slip in one direction. Once we have realised this, it means we can actively work at balancing it back out.

LIFE IN THE AMAZON JUNGLE

Chapter 9

Life in the Amazon Jungle

Bolivia

AMBER

One of the first things I had planned to do after I landed in Bolivia's largest city, Santa Cruz, was to buy a Spanish handbook as absolutely no one spoke English! This was a new one for me. Bolivia is a Spanish-speaking country, and I was a little unprepared with my impulsive decision to go there, knowing little-to-no Spanish. When I tried to say the name of the place I was heading to, no one could understand me. I thought I was pronouncing it as the locals would, but they looked at me like I was an alien or talking gibberish. Unable to check the internet because there was no phone service, I resorted to sign language, which was a real struggle, but it gave me a few good laughs with the locals.

Eventually, I found someone who understood what I was trying to say. This local guy worked out I was trying to get to the animal sanctuary, so he showed me to one of the rapiditos (minivans that provide public transport much faster than buses) at what looked like a bus station. Rapiditos are never in the best shape and, often, seemed to only just be holding together. The rapidito was loaded up to the brim with way too many people (a lot more people than seats) and a pile of large bags was stacked high on the roof. The driver indicated we were in for a five-hour journey, but I was excited I was finally heading to the Amazon jungle! Well, I was at least 80 per cent sure that's where we were headed.

After a very squished and dodgy three-hour journey on a dusty, bumpy road in sweltering heat with no air-con, it started to get dark. Several times, I thought we'd broken down, or at the very least popped a tyre, after hitting potholes way too fast, but to my surprise we carried on as if it was normal.

The driver stopped at random places along the road to let people off the rapidito. They were all locals, very friendly and, from what I could make out, likely farmed the large open fields we were driving past.

Eventually, we came up to a very small town where the driver indicated for me to hop out. I was puzzled. I had seen a road sign with the town's name on it and, although I couldn't pronounce the name, I was sure it wasn't my stop.

Through sign language, I managed to explain this to the driver, but he insisted and then pointed me to a group of minivans all parked up at what must have been the town taxi point. I finally understood what he meant and got out of the van as the driver grabbed my bag off the roof.

Now that it was dark, I was pretty keen to keep going and get to my destination. There were a lot of busy locals around, all hustling and bustling and wheeling and dealing around a ticket booth. There was dust in the air, dingy but charming little food stalls everywhere (which I would come to love) and plenty of general confusion, although that might just have been on my part!

After a lot of going back and forth at the ticket booth, I managed to catch another dubious little van. The driver had signalled he knew where the animal sanctuary I was heading to was, as he regularly dropped off people there.

After what felt like a very long time, but was probably an hour and a half, on an even bumpier road, the driver pulled over and indicated that this was my stop. I jumped out, grabbed my bag and stood on the side of the road. Through the darkness I could just make out thick jungle in front of me. I was a little hesitant, but then the driver pointed towards a sign before he drove off.

I crossed the road and shone my torch on the sign — written on it was the park's name. I was in the right place. Woohoo!

My excitement soon faded as I stared into the dark jungle. It wasn't very reassuring that there were no lights or noise from all the people I thought would be here. I dragged my suitcase down the driveway in the pitch black, still wondering if I was in the right place.

In the jungle, I found a small, wooden hut with a thatched roof and a dirt floor, but no lights and no people. I tried calling out … nothing. How strange. There were supposed to be loads of people here, but instead it was eerily quiet. With growing dread, I looked around and listened to the insects chirp, leaves swish and branches break in the dark jungle.

Just when I was beginning to think I was in the wrong place and was considering turning around and getting the hell out as quickly as I could, an Aussie girl came out of one of the huts and welcomed me. It was great to hear a voice and as a bonus it spoke English, which I could understand!

I had turned up on the one night everyone had gone to the closest town, which consisted of only about six huts, for a feed and some beers. Just my luck.

I was shown to one of the huts that had a spare bed. Wow! I was certainly in the jungle now. There were no luxury items, such as a floor, proper walls, lights or even a mattress. This was going to be interesting!

The park consisted of about 10 huts, which were the living quarters for anywhere between 15 and 60 people, depending on how many volunteers were there at the time. These huts had thatched roofs and the walls were wood up to about waist height. Where the low walls finished, there was wire mesh going up to the roof to prevent animals from getting in, which gave a new meaning to the term open-plan living. The floor was bare earth, although two of the fancier huts – we jokingly called them the 'Gucci' huts – had concrete floors, and each hut had two or three bunk beds with straw mattresses.

After a surprisingly solid night's sleep, I woke to the chirping of monkeys. From my straw mattress, I could see straight out through the mesh to the trees above where monkeys were swinging around. I'd never seen anything like it – this was epic!

This animal sanctuary is, probably, the most outrageously awesome place to work; however, there is certainly nothing glamorous about it. The living conditions were rough, the food was minimal and there were only the very basic necessities available, but I think this was all part of its charm. The thing I loved most about it was that, as an animal sanctuary (and unlike a zoo), it was there for the good of the animals not people.

The park took in hurt, abused or struggling exotic jungle animals, and gave them fulfilling lives. If possible, these animals would be released back into the wild once they were fit and healthy enough. Working there as a volunteer, I only ever got to meet the animals I worked with. This was to give the animals as much of a natural 'wild' life as possible while they were being looked after and nursed back to health.

Some of these poor animals had suffered cruel fates before being rescued by the park. A lot of these animals were taken from people who had bought them on the black-market thinking, 'How cute will it be to have a baby puma running around?' Unfortunately, when the baby puma grows up, these same people now have a wild, dangerous and no longer cute mountain lion locked up in their tiny houses with humans.

One poor jaguar rescued by the park had been kept on a 2-metre metal chain under a house for its whole life, only being fed scraps every now and then. This jaguar was very malnourished and in extremely bad shape and required a lot of attention to get him back to health. Another jaguar was half blind, with almost crippled hind legs, after someone had attempted to get rid of their pet with a flame thrower after it had grown big and was no longer a cute cub.

Some of the monkeys at the park had been rescued by locals after large companies had come through and felled big swathes of the Amazon jungle, destroying everything in their path, including many animals for which the jungle was home. Sadly, the Amazon jungle is still disappearing at an alarming rate.

I arrived at the end of dry season and the park was at half-capacity for volunteers. There were about 35 of us, which was enough people to have fun with but not so many that it was crowded. This also meant I was assigned two different species of animals to look after. I had my heart set on working with the big cats – jaguars and pumas – as I was naturally drawn to them, but we didn't get to choose which we worked with and were instead assigned to whatever animals needed help at the time. I was assigned to three baby howler monkeys in the mornings and two puma sisters in the afternoons. In hindsight, this was a blessing, and I couldn't have chosen better.

Those three howler monkeys were an absolute ball! These little critters were so much fun and they sure kept me on my toes. I was meant to work with the howler monkeys for two weeks before being rotated on to take care of other animals, but I had such an incredible time with these guys that I ended up looking after them for a month.

In the mornings, I would set out across the jungle and find my way to the howler monkeys' enclosure. All the animals were kept in separate areas of the jungle, so they didn't cross each other's paths or territories. Lucho was the biggest male, and while he was very playful he was also a little aggressive towards other monkeys. The other male, Luas, was the smallest of the three. He was so little and cute but tended to be a bit whiney sometimes. All Luas wanted to do was snuggle, and he'd act really innocent and sweet, and then he'd sneakily wind up the others. The female monkey, Sabrina, was medium-sized and very independent. She always did her own thing and was not fussed about the other two. On my first day, she took my finger innocently – and then bit it. I think she was trying to communicate her first impressions of me, which weren't great straight off the bat. Thankfully, this changed over time and we ended up with a tight bond.

Each time I got into their enclosure, I would swing open the mesh doors and the monkeys would jump all over me to say hello. We would then walk through the jungle, with the three of them either riding on my shoulders or following along in the trees above. Once we got to a good tree, we would all go climbing. I had an absolute ball climbing trees with these monkeys. Some of the other volunteers commented on how my hair was the same colours as the monkeys' so they probably thought I was their mother!

The first time we climbed together, all three of them stopped in the tree to watch me, looking puzzled, like I was the monkey. I guess other volunteers usually stood on the ground and watched them play instead of climbing into the trees with the monkeys. I loved climbing, but also wanted to keep them off the ground as much as possible, as in the wild, that's where the predators are.

The trees were so much taller than I was used to, and they all had vines hanging off them, which made climbing them much easier. Luas had a habit of hanging off me while I climbed. It's surprising how much more difficult it is to climb a tree with a monkey hanging around your neck! At the top of the tree, I would find a little possie to sit, and they would go off and play in the nearby branches, before coming back to lie on my lap, wrestle with each other or play with me.

At lunchtime, I would take them back to their enclosure and feed them. I hid food all over their cage, which kept them entertained for hours.

One morning, I was sitting high up in a tree as the monkeys disappeared for a few hours, playing in the jungle canopy. As I sat there on a large branch, minding my own business, I heard something come crashing through the trees. It sounded a lot bigger than my little howler monkeys.

I looked in the direction of the noise and saw a wild large-headed capuchin monkey popping out of the jungle, landing on a branch on the tree next to me. He was a *big* alpha male. These monkeys are mean looking and have a reputation to match. They are very hostile, particularly the big males, and when we were walking through the jungle, they often threw things at us while jumping up and down aggressively.

This big alpha male just sat on his branch, eyeballing me. It was a real stare down. He didn't even blink! With no other choice, I accepted his challenge and stared back at him without blinking either. I was suddenly very aware that I was more than 10 metres off the ground with no easy or quick escape route.

As I stared back at this big alpha male, out of the corner of my eye, I noticed another monkey pop out of nowhere. I lost the staring competition as I broke my concentration to look over at the newcomer … then another monkey popped out … then a fourth and a fifth … Pretty soon, I was surrounded by 42 of the little buggers! They were above me, below me, on each side of me – all around me. There were seven large males and the rest were smaller males, females and even some babies.

Although they were a lot smaller than me, I got the feeling that if it was going to be 42 against one, the 42 would likely win. Heck, just one of the big males could probably take me out. The capuchins above me started to get pretty close, and the big males weren't mucking around either. They began to be daring and aggressive as they jumped up and down on their branches before swinging across the branches and doing mock charges at me while shrieking and showing their large fangs.

I was pretty keen to get out of their way before one of them followed through with their charge, but I knew that, as with most wild animals in the jungle, if you run, they'll chase you!

The best way to go about it was for me to slowly move off while not looking like I was backing down. I stood up on my branch then shuffled my way across to the next branch. The buggers swung across and cut me off. Unbelievable!

They'd sensed my plan and, with a rustle and a shriek, four of the monkeys swung across to the branch I was heading for, then stared at me while showing their fangs. Eeek! I was in a little bit of a pickle.

The ground was a long way down, probably too big a drop for me to survive, so plan B was to intimidate them by acting bigger and more aggressive than they were. This can work pretty well, although you have to be ready if it backfires and they don't back down. They looked like they were about to rip me apart. I searched around for anything I could use for self-defence if they charged any closer. I broke off a branch and stood ready. The tension in the air was crazy. I could tell they were seconds off from attacking.

Just as things were about to come to a head, out of nowhere, my three howler monkeys came swinging across the jungle canopy and bowled straight through the capuchin monkeys to jump all over me. Once they saw what was happening, they turned to face the capuchins. With bullet-proof confidence, they charged at a group of them to one side, who quickly scattered. The howlers then made their way around the other small groups of capuchins and charged at them. Then all three would choose an individual and gang up on one capuchin at a time, then scare them off. Holy heck, I was impressed!

These guys sure as hell had my back and it was amazing to watch. They were much smaller than the capuchins, but they were bold as anything and didn't hesitate.

Pretty soon, most of the females, babies and juvenile males had scattered off into the jungle, and it was only the big male capuchins left staring us out. With the rest of their crew gone now, I could tell these big capuchins had lost the puff out of their fight. The look in their eyes had changed from raw aggression to defeated hatred. One by one, they moved off, and I was left standing on my branch at the top of a tree feeling bewildered by what had just happened. My thoughts were soon interrupted as my three howler monkeys jumped all over me playfully, chattering and chirping to each other like it was just a normal day.

In the afternoons at the park, I would go out to a different area of the jungle with two other volunteers to look after the puma sisters, Wara and Yassi. Having two pumas together like this was very unusual as pumas are solitary animals, with each of them occupying a large patch of jungle as their territory. These puma sisters, however, always stayed together. If one wouldn't walk, neither of them would walk. They had to go everywhere together, which was kind of cute.

Wara was the largest puma at the park, and with her very green eyes she looked just like a big lioness. (Pumas are mountain lions after all.) She had a very nice nature but was unpredictable when she got excited. Yassi was a little smaller than Wara, but she made up for her lack of size in attitude. Even though she was the smaller of the pair, Yassi was the dominant puma. She was the catty one and she would try to scrap with Wara all the time. Yassi would keep me alert by nipping at my knees with her sharp teeth, just to let me know she could.

Each afternoon, the three of us would head to the pumas' enclosure. To say hello, we'd put our hands through the fence and let the pumas lick our arms to pick up our scent. After the greeting, we would then enter the enclosure. Each of the pumas would stand on their own wooden platform and purr so loudly they sounded like revving lawnmowers. We would take turns to give each of them a good scratch around the ears, a belly rub, and – once I had a close bond with them – a head rub too. The pumas loved to rub their faces on our faces and necks in a snuggly sort of way, and they were the only pumas in the park that did this.

Each puma wore a collar onto which we would hook their leash so we could take them out of their enclosure to walk through the jungle for enrichment. While that might sound as easy as taking your dog for a walk, there was a little more to it. There was a special way to do everything both to ensure we were safe and so that the best interests of the cats were met.

We always let the pumas do what they wanted; the walk was totally theirs. If they stopped and sat down or slept, we sat with them and waited as quietly as we could. When they got up and carried on, so did we, and if they took off running, we ran after them. Running after them often involved one of us getting dragged off our feet before coming to a screeching halt as we tripped on something like a tree root and face planted!

Yassi was always keen for a walk but, sometimes, we would have to tempt Wara with blades of grass to get her walking. Can you believe that? Blades of grass, of all things! A single blade of grass was enough to tempt a puma into a walk.

Each puma would have one volunteer walking it, while the third person walked in between them in case there were any issues, and we rotated these roles between the three of us. Usually, pumas of this size would need to be walked using a double-rope system, which is what we used for the jaguars. This is where they would have two separate ropes attached to their collar and they would be walked by two people. That way, if the puma or jaguar started to give you their stalking eyes or their play got a little feisty, the walkers could split their ropes and stand on either side of the animal. Tension can then be put on the leash to hold the animal off the person if need be.

These pumas were so well behaved (mostly) that we only used one rope on each of them, but it did mean they could turn and jump on us if they were feeling playful.

As with many of the big cats at the park, this was a regular part of their play and they didn't intend it to be aggressive. If this happened, we were taught to act as boringly as possible: no sudden movement, no excitement, no yelling, nothing, until they lost interest and turned their attention to something else. On the odd occasion, if they kept going, we were told to bunch our hand up and put a fist in their mouth, which they would half-heartedly gnaw on for a while until they got bored.

Can you imagine standing there as a jaguar or puma is casually chewing your arm and doing nothing about it, or putting your fist in their mouth of all places? A person's natural instinct is either fight or flight when threatened, both of which would get the big cat more excited and turn playing into 'not playing'. During my time at the sanctuary, it became very natural to just stand there and take it when one of these big cats decided to toy with me. Then we'd go back to camp at the end of the day, and everyone would share their battle stories.

There are a few key rules to follow with these big cats to ensure playing stays playing. One is that you never want to be smaller than them, so if I fell over, I would slowly and methodically get back on my feet. It was also important to always let them know I could see them. If they thought I wasn't looking, they'd see it as a good stalking opportunity.

Another rule is to never let the puma get behind you or get on your back, which they always try to do. When a puma goes for its prey, it goes for their back and then, eventually, strikes with a powerful bite to the neck. A jaguar also goes for the back, but, instead of the neck, it crushes the skull of its prey – jaguars have the strongest jaws in the whole of the cat kingdom. This hunting instinct is why you'd never want either of them getting on your back.

Once the pumas were out of their enclosure, the walk was at their own pace and they chose which trails we took. One of the benefits of walking two pumas together was that they could play and stalk each other (instead of us). It was quite comical at times. While it was blatantly obvious they could see each other and us, they pretended to be sneaky and still stalk one another.

A typical scene that played out was that one of the other volunteers would be up the front with Yassi, with me and Wara coming up the trail behind them. Yassi would then leave the trail and hide about two metres off in the trees. Wara knew Yassi was in the bush and would keep walking up the trail, slowly and cautiously, while closely watching the leaves next to the trail for any potential threat. Yassi, with her big stalking eyes on, would be crouching in the bush, rear legs cocked and ready to pounce. The suspense would build until, finally, Yassi would jump out at Wara, then they would wrestle and fight until one of them sprinted off, dragging one of us with them. Even though they weren't going for us, we were roped to them and the tension was still enough to get the blood pumping!

Most of their trails led to a river, where we would sit on the bank for half an hour before walking (or sprinting) back.

On my very first walk with Wara, I was unprepared when she took off in a sprint halfway back to the enclosure. Of course, this happened right where we had to weave through some trees. My gumboots were about three sizes too big so as I sprinted after her I couldn't get through the trees quick enough. Splat! I fell head over heels and got dragged along for a few metres before Wara stopped and looked back. I jumped to my feet (a little bruised and battered and not wanting to stay on the ground for long as it meant I was an easy target for the puma), then we sprinted all the way to the enclosure.

Back at the enclosure, it was feeding time. We clipped the pumas to their platforms, and they'd be given either a delightful bowl of chicken foot and chunky meat soup or big slabs of raw meat. The meat slabs were the best to feed them. We would stand a few metres away from their platform, call out 'uno, dos, tres!' while swinging the meat to the count and, on 'tres', we'd throw the meat slab for them to catch. It was very impressive watching them grab the meat out of the air.

Yassi would twitch with each count, then on 'tres', she would jump up on her hind legs and grab the meat with her front paws – she looked just like a dangerous but cute teddy bear. Meanwhile, Wara was a beast. On 'tres', she would jump up on her hind legs and swat the meat out of the air with one powerful paw, looking like a boxer landing a king hit. When they were being fed, Wara's purr sounded just as you would expect a large cat to sound, but Yassi's was bizarre, like some kind of dinosaur screeching – loud and intense.

The weather could have a big effect on these beautiful big cats. Most days, it was stinking hot in the jungle, so the pumas were sleepy and lethargic in the heat of the day and most active at night. As we came into the wet season, they were totally different in cooler weather. They had loads of energy and could be a little unpredictable, so I really needed to have my wits about me.

When storms hit, in the space of about two minutes it could go from hot, sunny weather to torrential rain with wind thrashing the trees around. If we happened to be out walking a big cat when this happened, it was in our best interest to get back to their enclosure as soon as possible because they could go a little crazy when the thunder, lightning and wind frightened them.

On my first rainy day at the sanctuary, as soon as we got to their enclosure, the puma sisters were already chasing each other around and having a hell of a good time. They had more energy than usual, so it was going to be an exciting day.

Once we got them on their leashes, Wara was eager to explore, so she and I pulled away in front, leaving the others trailing behind us. We got to a corner of the trail that had thick bushes off to one side. My puma paused for a moment before leaving the trail and walking into the bushes. I fed her leash out to its full length and stayed on the trail.

Just three metres from me, the puma sat looking back at me, which was pretty normal, although the other puma would usually be closer behind for her to stalk. The others weren't far behind us, so I wasn't concerned. But as Wara sat hidden in the shoulder-height leaves, she started looking at me with her big stalking eyes. Uh oh! I felt the tension in her gaze change from a passive stare to intense concentration as her black pupils enlarged. I was suddenly very aware of how fast my heart was beating. As casually as possible, I snapped off a whole lot of leaves, so I could clearly see her and so she couldn't pretend she was concealed. I said her name loudly while I looked straight at her so she knew I could see her and I wasn't having a bar of her games. Unfortunately, this didn't deter her. Wara had slowly moved into a crouching position and was getting ready to pounce. I knew this puma was serious and there was nothing I could do to distract her.

With my adrenaline pumping, I took a step towards her and held my ground, so she'd have less of a run-up and would pack less of a punch if she did strike. I called out to the other two, to let them know my puma was stalking me so they could be ready.

It was astonishing to see how quickly this puma could go from looking like a large, cuddly domestic cat to a terrifying predator that could rip me to pieces without even trying. Her pupils covered her whole eyes, making her look like an angry lioness. Her hind legs were tensioned, ready to spring, straining under her slightly raised rear, and her chest was low over her front paws. She was ever so slightly shifting her weight from side to side with anticipation as she posed ready to pounce. The building suspense was wild and I took a deep breath as it drew out for a few very long seconds.

Her head dipped slightly and ears went back, her enormous eyes concentrated on me and she zeroed in, then … Wham!

Quicker than the eye could see, with one powerful launch, she was on me. The puma pounced on me with the full force of an excited mountain lioness, and I stood face on to her with one arm in front of me, bent at the elbow to keep her off my body. I felt like I'd just been rugby tackled. I resisted her force and stood braced while offering her my arm to discourage her from latching on to any other part of me.

She stood on her hind legs, which made her the same height as me, and she dug her claws into my shoulder and playfully but firmly bit my arm – thankfully, I was wearing a thick long-sleeved top which bore the brunt of her teeth.

Usually, that was the extent of it when the pumas jumped like this; they would then hop down and casually walk off as if nothing had happened. To them, this was just play and they didn't think they were being aggressive. However, in this instance, she was so excited because of the cool weather that she didn't stop there.

Amber and Serena doing some 4WDing, 1993. Older sister Chelsea is holding the fuel can at the back.

Amber caught a big snapper fishing with dad Gavin, 1997.

Amber, Serena and younger sister Jasmine making their own survival challenge in the mud, Waiuku, NZ, 2002.

Amber loaded into a Black Hawk helicopter on army deployment, serving in East Timor, 2009.

Scuba diving for crayfish off the east coast of New Zealand, 2016.

Serena about to solo skydive, hanging off the wing of a plane, Jurien Bay, Western Australia, 2013.

Serena carrying a deer out on a hunting trip, with Amber at the front, 2018.

Serena with her NZ-record mahi-mahi, 2016. Skipper Dad in the background.

Serena working at an underground gold mine, where she drove the dumptrucks, Kambalda, Western Australia, 2011.

Working as emergency services officers at open pit mines in the outback, Western Australia, 2013. Amber on medic duties and Serena fighting bushfires.

Mount Everest Base Camp, Nepal, 2014.

World's Highest Marathon finish line, Mount Everest, Nepal, 2014.

Amber and some of her team during the Eagle Cap Extreme Dog
Sled Race, Oregon, early 2015.

Snoopy resting in the sled, on the second afternoon of the race.

Amber snowboard 'joring', being pulled by some of the dog team, Michigan, early 2015.

Doing body-weight workouts on holidays without gym gear, 2018. Serena is lifting Amber.

Amber sailing from Hawai'i across the Pacific Ocean, mid 2015.

Amber walking with baby howler monkeys in the Bolivian jungle, late 2015.

Amber rubbing heads with one of the puma sisters, Bolivia, late 2015.

Amber with jaguar Katie, mid-jungle walk, Bolivia, late 2015.

Serena with Amber (below), climbing up steep rocks, Mount Cook (Aoraki), NZ, summer 2015–2016.

Serena ice climbing above the snow line on Mount Cook, summer 2015–2016.

Amber and Serena on the summit, Mount Cook, late 2017.

At a waterhole near the campsite, during *Naked and Afraid*, Limpopo, South Africa, 2019.

Breaking down meat with an arrowhead after a successful impala hunt – their first food in 8 days.

Amber and Serena setting a snare trap for a survival challenge.

Serena and Amber just before the luxury of the first shower after filming ends for *Naked and Afraid*.

Taking a break to enjoy the view, hiking the Lake Waikaremoana Great Walk, NZ, 2017.

Hiking Cape Brett, NZ, on a family rock fishing trip, 2019.

With her claw still in my shoulder, Wara looked up at me with her huge predator eyes, then she did the classic puma move of spinning around so she could get on my back. Usually, I would take a step and spin with her to avoid it, but the cunning little devil had chosen a clever spot as there was a tree in the way, so I couldn't turn around.

The advice to 'just spin with the animal so it can't get on your back' might sound simple, but it's not. You have to spin slowly enough not to excite the animal, but fast enough to stop it from thinking through the move and trapping you, while also preventing it from getting on your back. As I say, they are very cunning animals.

Without being able to spin around, the puma managed to get on my back without delay. Still trying to keep my cool and act as passively as possible about the situation, the thought 'don't let her get to my neck!' raced through my mind as I fought to stay on my feet.

Wara was behind me, still on her hind legs with one claw in each shoulder. She was chewing her way up my right shoulder, with each bite getting a little bit harder and I was very aware she was getting closer to my neck. I felt Wara's sharp claws dig into the back of my thighs as her hind legs jumped off the ground to latch onto the flesh on the back of my legs. She was now fully on me, trying to get me on the ground. My pants were much thinner than my thick canvas shirt, so I felt her claws more than her teeth.

The bites were hard but not vicious, and puma teeth are blunt so they don't break the skin – they just cause bruises. The claws, though, can be a little sharper. If I'd tried to throw her off, things might have played out differently. It was very strange to just stand there and let this happen, but if I did anything else, it would make the situation worse.

With the puma on my back, she had worked her bites up my shoulder almost to the base of my neck. Her huge jaws were close enough that I could smell the stench of rotten meat on her breath. This all felt like it was happening in slow motion. My heart was beating out of my chest as I bunched my left hand into a fist and put it over my right shoulder, using my right arm to push it as far behind my head as I could flex. The puma's mouth closed on my fist and I momentarily breathed out with relief that she'd gone for my fist and not my neck.

At the same time, one of the other volunteers came around the corner and froze so as not to excite the puma more.

She calmly asked if I needed help, and I told her to walk up casually and put her fist in the puma's mouth too. Before she could, Wara detached her claws from my flesh, jumped off me and stood in the middle of the trail. Whe-ew!

I was glad as hell the others had come around the corner when they did. I had a good few battle wounds to show everyone back at camp that day. My backpack saved my back but my jacket was torn to shreds. I had claw marks on my shoulders and legs, and bruises from the puma's teeth, but other than that I was unscathed.

It wasn't just the monkeys and the pumas that I had to keep an eye on out in the jungle. There were also the creepy crawlies, which weren't necessarily small. One morning, I was running down the road when I noticed a brown creature, the size of a small bird, sitting there sunbathing in the early morning warmth. I discovered it was a tarantula and was fascinated by this huge, hairy, eight-legged creature that had a bulging, egg-sized body and legs that stretched out to same size as my foot! As I stood staring at it, the spider started to move. When I took off, I was shocked to see it could run almost as fast as me!

The spiders had nothing on the ticks, which were constant, and not just on the animals but on us too. Every few days, I'd have to get someone to pick them off my back – they were the reason we wore long sleeves, pants and gumboots in the sweltering jungle heat. The ticks were horrendous, but my most hated insects were the yellow flies. Arrrrgh, I hate yellow flies! They are big, fat, feral flies that sting like a bee, causing large welt-like wounds. If you had any skin exposed, they would get you. I ended up having to wear socks to climb trees to stop the yellow flies from attacking my feet. If I climbed barefoot, by the time I got to the top of a tree, I would have about 10 bites on each foot and they would be swollen to pieces. I was fortunate enough not to experience botflies, which laid live larvae in the flesh of a few of the unlucky volunteers.

Making up for some of the uncomfortable challenges were the wonderful people I worked with. The park had a good crew of people who were all there for the same reason – to look after animals that couldn't fend for themselves. There were always a good few laughs and plenty of stories back at camp each evening after a day out with the animals.

One evening, I came into camp and everyone was buzzing and gossiping about a big creature out in the jungle. I grinned as I heard one of the guys tell the story of an encounter he'd had that day. He'd been out walking through the jungle when he'd heard something big up in a tree … then the whole tree began to shake as a mysterious large creature began to move through the branches. He'd gone to get a bit closer to see what it was when the wild beast had begun grunting and carrying on so that the whole tree swayed. He had thought better of it and turned around and got out of there pretty quickly.

As he told me the story, I laughed so hard I could barely stand up. When I could finally talk without cracking up, I let him know that the terrifyingly big, mysterious creature in the tree had been me! I'd been high up in the jungle canopy climbing with the monkeys when I noticed him walking through the jungle, so I decided to have some fun and started shaking the tree and making grunting noises. He was not too impressed!

After a month or so, and with volunteers coming and going, I was switched to other animals, which was bittersweet. I was excited to work with different animals but was also gutted to have to part with the baby howler monkeys and the puma sisters. Even if they did test me every now and again, it had been extremely rewarding looking after these animals and I'd grown quite attached to them.

For the next month, I would be spending my mornings looking after an ocelot and my afternoons looking after a jaguar. What an amazing combo!

Up until then, I'd never heard of an ocelot. It turns out they're felines that are smaller than jaguars but with the same spotty pattern on their coats.

The different cats in the park came with their different attributes, which I picked up pretty quickly as I spent time with them. The pumas were slim, fast, agile and built of lean muscle. Given they weighed about the same as I did, I felt as though I could hold my own when they launched at me. A jaguar, however, while still being fast and agile, had sheer bulk and weight behind their staunch but playful strikes. A puma launching at you was like getting hit by a sprinter coming out of nowhere, while a jaguar launching at you was more like getting hit by solid rugby player, which made it a lot harder to stay on your feet! With the jaguars being the biggest cats at the park, they could be rather intimidating – they have the strongest jaw muscles of all of the large cats and kill their prey by crushing their skull.

My morning ocelot was called Lucinda, known as Lucy. She was an energetic little thing the size of a small dog and she was, undoubtedly, the fiercest cat I worked with. Lucy had the sharpest little teeth and claws. I was glad she was small because she could be pretty lethal. Boy, did I know about it when she got me!

While the pumas had mainly been mellow with the odd playful burst of messing around, Lucy was permanently playful and only once in a blue moon was she mellow. As soon as I stepped into her enclosure, she would launch at me like a little firecracker. My first challenge was to get her collar on while she mauled me. Her tiny but vicious claws and sharp teeth kept my attention.

I had to be on constant watch while I was walking her as she would take any opportunity to claw her way up my legs and back until she was clinging to the back of my head if I didn't stop her in time. She was lightning fast so, despite my best efforts, this happened quite often.

Ocelots spend a lot of their time in trees rather than on the jungle floor. They are very skilled at climbing up and down trees and jumping from one to another, which almost makes them more like monkeys than cats.

I would let Lucy climb and have fun in the trees while feeding out her 4-metre rope, making sure she didn't get tangled. I had to watch her intently while she was climbing as she was prone to launching a surprise attack or two. She loved to wait until I least expected it, then launch herself out of a tree at my head and sink those sharp little teeth and claws into my shoulders. I learnt that the hard way, more than once.

Having spent my mornings with my ocelot, afternoons were spent walking a jaguar through the jungle with one of the other volunteers. When I first met my assigned jaguar, Katie, I was in absolute awe of her. Due to their size and power, jaguars were always walked by two people, each with their own leash so that, at any point, one walker could put tension on their leash to hold the jaguar off the other walker.

Once we made our way to Katie's territory in the jungle, the other volunteer and I would approach her enclosure and let her sniff and lick our hands. Her enclosure was a fenced off section of jungle that measured about a thousand square metres. Jaguar tongues are like sandpaper – they have grippy, pointy, little bumps, which are fine for a lick or two, but more than that is enough to graze your skin.

Once Katie had recognised us by our smell, we would walk to the end of her enclosure, clip the two ropes to her collar through the fence, take one rope leash each and then open the gate.

The first time I did this was exciting but also a little nerve-racking. As we opened the gate, Katie started to walk out of her enclosure. As she walked, her giant round, green, stalking eyes were fixed on me. She paused for half a second, tensioning her rear legs, getting all her weight ready then … Wham! She launched herself straight at me without hesitation. I didn't even have time to attempt to deter her or brace myself. She was testing the newbie all right. I managed to stay on my feet – just. She went straight into a second attempt to get me on the ground. It was certainly one way to get the old heart thumping, even if she was just playing around.

Once we'd got Katie out of her enclosure, we'd take her for a long walk through the jungle. She routinely started her walk by pausing outside her enclosure to greet us then eyeballing one of us to playfully pounce on. This jaguar really loved to push the boundaries, so after a few pounces, we would apply a bit of pressure on her leash, which was a signal to her that we were done playing around. After a few hours of walking, we would head back to her enclosure, feed her all sorts of raw meat goodies then head back through the jungle to camp.

There were many instances when our afternoon walk through the jungle turned into an exciting escapade. On one walk, we noticed our jaguar's ears prick up as she was alerted to something out in the jungle. We didn't hear a twig snap or even a rustle in the leaves, but she certainly did. All we knew was that one moment we were paused there with the jaguar alert and sniffing the air, then the next moment we'd been yanked clean off our feet!

A peccary, which is a kind of jungle pig, had crossed our path and the first we knew about it was when our ropes went tight and we were ripped forward as Katie bolted after it. The jaguar went from zero to a hundred in a split second and, more impressively, all while towing us. Holy heck was she powerful – and fast!

We both tried to sprint after her; we didn't want to hold her back, but she was way too fast for even our quickest sprints. As she boosted onwards, she half dragged us along behind her. As I watched the sheer force that drove her powerful stride, her bulky back and rump muscles bulging with each extension as she lunged forwards, I thought about how powerful this jaguar was and how I was glad I was not a peccary. With us both in tow, she eventually lost the scent of the peccary and gave up the chase. It was an entertaining afternoon alright.

For the next month and a half, my routine was to walk my gorgeous, fierce little ocelot in the morning, before heading back to camp for lunch, after which I'd go out for an afternoon walk with my beast of a jaguar, Katie. Life was grand! I was taking care of these incredible animals while living the simple life with no power, limited food, no hot water, no phones or internet, sleeping on a straw mattress in a hut with a mud floor.

After a couple of amazing months volunteering with these animals, it was time to move on. It was hard to leave them behind, but I knew there were more great people arriving every day to take care of them. The memories I had created with them will stay with me for life.

THE GOOD AND THE BAD

Going into an adventure, you never know what the outcome of the experience will be. After you have given it a good crack, you'll know whether you loved it and you'll do it again or whether it turned out to not be your cup of tea and you'll not likely ever want to do it another time. Regardless of which one it ends up being for you, I'm pretty sure it will create some priceless memories you will cherish.

Sometimes the most testing adventures with the most outrageous challenges end up creating your fondest memories (even if you would never do it again). It's the blood, sweat and tears that make you look back with pride and think, 'Wow! I can't believe I did that.'

If it turns out to be a good experience, your life is enriched, and your spirit comes alive with the excitement of the journey, making the little worries in life seem insignificant. However, we need the bad experiences too, otherwise how would we know when things are good?

If you are experiencing the bad, remember it is only a moment in time – it can't rain forever! You *will* get through it.

Our miserable experiences contrast with the amazing ones. They teach us to cherish how good the good times are and how wonderful the epic times are. It's through these experiences that you discover what you enjoy and, just as importantly, what you don't enjoy in life. They also help you to figure out which things you want to put more time and effort into and which things put you in a good place, both physically and mentally.

The good and the bad: both kinds of adventures give us perspective, shape us and prepare us for the next challenge … the next adventure … the next opportunity.

THE CLOUD PIERCER

Chapter 10

The Cloud Piercer

Mount Cook, NZ

SERENA

Our sights had been set on climbing the 'cloud piercer', Mount Cook (Aoraki), for a couple of years. Amber and I had climbed mountains overseas, but just the two of us climbing New Zealand's tallest mountain together was going to make this one unique and really special.

This is a serious mountain ascent that requires a high level of fitness, technical climbing skills and the ability to make quick judgement calls, which could be the difference between life and death. Even so, we were filled with excitement, determination and a healthy respect for the mountain. We trusted each other completely, which meant we were a confident climbing team, and we also had the same goal that trumps the excitement of the challenge – to return home in one piece!

Mount Cook is the country's highest mountain. Standing at 3724 metres, it dominates New Zealand's Southern Alps, which run down the spine of the South Island. The mountain is often underestimated, but its technical terrain, vertical ice and rock faces, large crevasses and avalanche risk mean it's no place for novices. It's rare for a season to go by without at least one fatality on Mount Cook.

The climbing season usually runs from November through to February, and we started our climb in late December so we would be on the mountain to greet the New Year. As this is the height of the New Zealand summer, the days were relatively long, which worked in our favour.

The majority of climbers who attempt the summit fly to Plateau Hut, which sits on the side of Mount Cook at an elevation of 1800 metres. Amber and I, however, decided to walk in alongside the Tasman River bed, on the south-eastern side of the mountain, not far from Mount Cook village.

There are no tracks or trails leading up the mountain, so we did a lot of research on the different routes and printed off some maps showing what to look for. The best we could find were just some pixelated pictures of the mountain, but that would have to do as our map.

We got to the Mount Cook visitor carpark midafternoon and set off down a narrow 4WD track in our barely holding together, little rental car. That in itself was an adventure! We bounced, rolled and thudded over the track, which was made up of continuous rocks, scraping past the overgrown scrub. We'd slowly nudge up to rocks, getting on just the right angle, both of us cringing as we went over them, holding our breath as we waited to get bellied … and with a bang and a ding from underneath, we kept going until, finally, we got to a narrow river crossing with knee-high rocks. We knew we couldn't push the old rental over that. After squeezing our magical beast of a car off the trail and into some prickly shrub, we gathered our gear, ready to set off.

We threw our overflowing packs on our backs and hiked and boulder-hopped for a good few hours along Tasman Valley, trailing beside Tasman Glacier to Ball Hut, which sits near where Ball Glacier joins to Tasman Glacier. The hut is basic, with bunks for three people and a long-drop toilet.

The following morning, we got up at a sparrows fart and got straight into a quick brew to warm us, coffee for Amber and tea for me, then porridge for breakfast. Wide awake and full of excitement, we set off into the darkness at 5 am. Our plan was to head up the steep rocky banks towards Boys Glacier, then make our way around to Cinerama Col before crossing Grand Plateau to arrive at Plateau Hut.

Through dew-soaked tussock, we trekked along the edge of Tasman Glacier until the goat track we had been following came to a grinding halt and the earth dropped away. The drop-off appeared to be the only way to go, so we searched around for a route down it.

We dropped over a ridge of loose, gravel-like rocks. At the bottom of the 10-metre bank, we found ourselves standing on the edge of the glacier. Instead of it being white or blue with hard ice, it was grey and covered in rocks ranging in size from boulders as big as a truck down to pebbles.

A couple of hours of continual boulder-hopping proved difficult for us in our bulky, oversized, rigid mountaineering boots, which were designed for snow and not rocks. Although unsuitable for boulder-hopping, these boots would be ideal in the snow and, because our packs were already heavier than we would have liked, carrying another pair of boots was not an option.

We felt like we were scrambling over the rocks at a good pace, but every time we looked up, we seemed to have barely moved. A little shocked by how long it was taking us to cover this section, and unsure whether we'd hiked far enough across the glacier, we decided to start heading up the mountain.

I looked at my watch in disbelief – we'd been moving for almost four hours and we'd only just made it off the glacier. According to the research we had done, we thought it would take us between 8 and 12 hours to get to Plateau Hut. We would later find out that those timings were for climbers who had had their gear ferried to the hut via helicopter.

Not long into our ascent, my tongue was already dry and sticky, and it was hard not to think about my burning thirst. I looked over at Amber and could tell by the look on her face that she was feeling the same.

Earlier that morning, there'd been a chill in the spring air, which had made the tips of my fingers numb, but now there wasn't a hint of that chill left and a roaring heat enveloped us. I could see a shimmering heat haze coming off the rocky terrain as the sun shone down from the blue, cloudless sky. The rocks beneath our feet radiated an earthy smell and our nostrils filled with the dust that had been disturbed by our progress.

While all our focus was on the task at hand, spectacular views of the snow-capped mountain range stretched as far as the eye could see in every direction. The whiteness of the snow made for a remarkable colour contrast from the black rock and yellow-green tussock below the snow line.

As well as the odd boulder, the mountain face was made up of loose rock and scree that crumbled in our hands when we grabbed at it, sending it tearing down the mountain. Every few minutes, there was a deep, echoing boom that would stop us in our tracks. We would scan the surrounding mountains until we identified where the rock fall was coming from, then we thanked our lucky stars it hadn't come from above us.

The sun was beating down, turning our cheeks rosy-red, but the glisten of excitement in our eyes remained strong. The beads of sweat that rolled down our foreheads soon dried up as we pushed past the point of dehydration, using everything we had to fight the urge to drink another ration of what was left of our water. Due to the weight of our packs, we carried just two litres of water each, which only needed to last us until we made it to the snow line. We were not even halfway there and we had just less than half our water left. I felt like I could easily drink double that amount without it even touching the sides.

We remained very conscious of time, so we didn't stop. Now 7 hours in, we had come to terms with our earlier suspicions that it would be at least a 16-hour day before we made it to the hut. Momentum was key, as we both knew things would get harder once the sun set and we'd have to navigate in the darkness.

Slowly, we climbed higher, clinging to the crumbling rock faces and scree, working out the climbable routes as we went. We leaned forwards to counter the weight of our 30-kilogram packs as we slogged up the mountain. On the near vertical sections, we used a system that involved one of us being a runner. Amber and I roped ourselves together, then whichever one of us was being the runner at the time would drop her pack and climb up to a boulder big enough to support our weight. She would then tie our rope off on the boulder.

Once the runner had completed her part, we would rig our rope into a pulley system to winch the packs up to the top of the boulder, as it was pretty much impossible to climb these vertical faces without getting ripped back down the slope under the weight of our packs. We took turns being the runner, but Amber took to it more naturally.

Often, the rocks we were climbing would move or dislodge as we passed, so we didn't have anything sturdy enough to tie off our rope to. When this happened, the runner would improvise and tie the rope off to themselves before digging in their feet behind a sizeable rock.

The runner's whole body would be under extreme tension from the effort as they free-climbed up, clinging to the near-vertical rocks, not daring to ease their muscles even a little until they reached a safe-enough boulder. One wrong move, one momentary lapse in concentration, or too much weight on your foot or hand-hold and it could be all over in such unforgiving terrain.

At one stage, Amber was halfway through climbing up a vertical crack in the rocks, while I was only just balancing below her, wedged in the crack where she had left her pack. I hoped she was going to tie off soon before my grip fatigued or my hand-hold gave way.

As she climbed, her rigid boots hardly made contact with the rock as they didn't flex at all and were too bulky to fit in any gaps. Only about two centimetres of the toe of her boot made contact with the rock. As she stretched out for her next hand-hold, there was a crack and a rumble as the rock gave way. She managed to scramble for a new grip and spread her weight evenly over four points of contact so as not to put too much stress on one point. From below, all I heard was a crack and a rumble, then her voice yelling, 'ROOOCKS!'

Unfortunately, as I was wedged in the crack below her, with a steep drop on either side, I couldn't move. I don't know how I fluked the timing, but while balancing there, I managed to lift a hand and then a foot just in time to let the showering rock fragments hurl past, picking up momentum as they went – well, all but one of them.

Despite my best efforts to dodge it, a golf-ball-sized rock hit me smack on the wrist. It felt as though I had been hit with a sledgehammer and I gasped at the pain. It took a few minutes to shake it off and get the feeling back in my hand, but I was thankful it hadn't been worse.

With each passing hour, our longing for water became more apparent. This wasn't helped when an apple managed to fly out of one of the packs and bounce down the slope, never to be seen again. Some mountain goat was going to have a very tasty snack! An apple doesn't sound like a big thing to lose, but with limited water on a boiling hot day and our mouths dry with a coating of thick dust, the thought of losing a refreshing apple was devastating.

Stunned for a minute as the juicy apple flew out of sight, we looked at each other and burst out laughing at the irony of losing an apple of all snacks. After having a good laugh, we carefully winched up the pack the rest of the way, conscious of the fact that a shovel was dangling from it. The shovel was a very important piece of equipment – it would be vital if we got caught in an avalanche, so we really couldn't afford to lose it.

Once at the top of that climb, we sat on a boulder to catch our breath and take on some food to refuel. We had been going for eight hours straight and the last couple of hours had been spent pushing ourselves to our limits. We allowed ourselves a mouthful of our remaining water, scoffed down some sweets and shared our remaining apple. Even though we were hungry, we couldn't eat anything substantial as our mouths were too parched to produce enough saliva to swallow the muesli bars, crackers, cheese and salami we'd brought for lunch. We reckoned we were about three quarters of the way up to the snow line where we would be able to melt snow to replenish our water supplies.

As we sat there, we took in the views around us. To finally be here on this great mountain made us grin from ear to ear. The mountains seemed to go forever and we didn't take up even a tiny speck of them. Here, my mind could run free. As we looked down at where we had come from, our progress gave us a spike of energy and made us eager to carry on. After a 15-minute rest, we set off for the snow line, which was about halfway to the hut.

On the steepest parts of the climb, we had to winch up our packs. They took a real hammering as they were bounced, dragged, ripped and hooked over the jagged rocks. If they got stuck, we had to lower them down a little, then swing them around the offending rock before continuing to hoist them up. This burnt a lot of time, so we decided to try abseiling.

Instead of winching up our packs, once the runner had tied off the rope, the second climber would climb up with her pack, using the rope as assistance, then abseil back down to bring up their own pack. This was much faster than winching up our packs but came at the cost of burning more energy.

We moved as fast as we could, mindful of time slipping away. Even so, I took a moment to look down towards where we had come from, which gave my spirits a little boost. The valley floor looked tiny in the distance.

After a few more hours of tough climbing and dodging flying rocks, the sun lost its punch. Having had our heads down hard at work for so long, excitement surged when we realised we were only metres away from the snow line.

Twelve hours in, we finally made it to the snow, and the altered terrain recharged the fire in our eyes. Our faces were blackened from the dust off the rocks and we had only a few mouthfuls of water left, which we decided to drink, as we knew we could now heat snow whenever we wanted.

It was starting to get late, so we decided we needed to gun it in order to make it to the hut before darkness set in. We tied our crampons onto our boots and, wearing our harnesses, we roped up to each other and got out our ice axes. The gleaming white snow looked rock hard, but under the weight of us and our packs, our crampons punched through the crusted top layer and we sunk in, with snow up to our knees. With our bodies feeling every part of the day's climb, our minds had to take over.

With our crampons on and ice axes in hand, we remained roped together the whole time we were on the snow face, which meant if one of us was to fall, the other one could self-arrest to stop us both from hurtling down the slope. Self-arresting involves quickly throwing yourself to the ground and digging your ice axe and crampons into the snow as hard as possibly, acting like an anchor in order to stop the fall.

Roped together with a 15-metre gap between us, we traversed up the first slope diagonally. Moving forwards took enormous amounts of energy for the lead climber, who had to punch through the snow. The second climber would then follow in the lead climber's footprints, which made it a little easier for them. We switched positions often so that neither of us ended up too exhausted.

At one point, we were heading down for a stretch to get past a steep knoll. Amber was leading when she disappeared over a waist-high ice bank. Before I could get completely over to the ice bank, I heard her call out, 'Falllllling!'

I hit the deck and self-arrested before the rope could go taut. As I lay on the slope, using all my weight to dig in my ice axe and crampons, my harness jolted violently as the rope went taut. It had caught Amber's weight.

Once she got back her footing, we got up and regrouped. 'Your drills were on point, mate!' she said. 'The rope pulled tight before I could even get my ice axe up.'

By now, the deep roar of falling rocks had been replaced by high-pitched cracks, followed by bellowing rumbles as masses of ice broke off, causing distant avalanches. We identified the safest route to take to avoid ice falls and avalanches as much as possible, but there were places where a high-risk route could not be avoided.

In one of these, we had to get around a section below a huge overhang of ice and rock. We had to move fast because if anything was to break off, we wouldn't survive to tell the tale. We moved so lightly and quickly you would have thought we were fresh, just having started out for the day. Once we were well clear of the overhang, the exhaustion came back and our feet felt even heavier than before.

After almost 16 hours on our feet, we pressed our way up yet another stretching slope then scraped over the ridge at the top. Then we followed a rocky cliff around until we were greeted by the view of a wide glacier. Above the glacier, there was a steep climb up to another snowy ridge with cliffs on each side.

Our spirits rose as we recognised that this was Cinerama Col. Up until now, we thought we were roughly on the right route, but now this had been confirmed. As the last traces of light reflected dimly off the snow, we grinned at each other — we were on track!

Our water had long since run out, but we were spurred on thinking the hut couldn't be far off. We would have plenty of time for water at the hut.

Even though we were surrounded by snow, the evening air felt warm. As we crossed the valley, we sank to our waists in the soft snow, our packs holding us down. The warm weather had caused massive crevasses to open up and they scarred the white blanket all around us. Crevasses can be hard to spot at times and, as their edges are unstable, they were just waiting to cave in. If either of us was to tread too close to one or miss seeing one that was about to open up, who knows how deep we would have been swallowed up.

Up and up we went, climbing as the darkness crept in and encased us. It was 10 pm and, having climbed over several false summits, our morale had taken a few little blows. We finally admitted we couldn't continue without water, and we'd done nearly six hours of intense physical climbing since our last mouthful. We stopped and kicked at the snow to form a platform on the steep bank, then we ripped out our gas cooker and pot and began the important task of melting snow. We sculled the resulting water as soon as the snow had melted. Water had never tasted so sweet!

Once we'd drunk our fill, we melted more snow to fill our bottles. We took a minute to grab our head torches, put on some warmer clothes to stop the shivering that the darkness had brought with it and refuelled with a very late lunch. We added some water to our dry-mix smoothies and scoffed down a generous helping of thick cheese and salami on crackers.

As we ate, we studied the dimly lit mountain above us and agreed that we'd need to be extra cautious now it was dark, as there would be hidden dangers, like crevasses, that we'd be unable to see.

Having studied the map and the contours of the mountain, we were confident enough that we would be able to continue on in the darkness. However, we were well aware that even the most skilled navigators can go off course in the dark of night. We contemplated digging in to bivvy up for the night but decided we couldn't be far from the hut. Packing away our gear, we checked our ropes and harnesses, heaved our packs back on our backs and continued on.

Amber and I seem to have an automatic default that when one of us feels tired or low on morale the other automatically becomes stronger, pushing us both on. In an instant, this can switch between us.

Night had set in and, as we looked up, we could just make out the white fall of the mountain face. It was nudging on midnight as we climbed on top of the peak for which we'd been aiming. Under my breath, I swore to myself, annoyed that my dull head torch only lit a 10-metre arc in the pitch black.

As we crossed over the snowy pass with cliffs on each side, the terrain changed and we headed slightly downhill. We felt a rush of relief and were thrilled at the thought of having a break from the steep inclines.

Below us was a vast open area, which was bound to have several ways to pass through. Our tiny head torch beams did nothing to light up a route, so we stopped, threw down our packs and sat on them. We stared out at the huge, open nothingness.

Under the barely detectable torch glow off the snow, we could just make out the huge mountains on each side of the massive, craterous dish in front of us. It was clearly riddled with crevasses and melting ice bridges.

Amber and I discussed whether to go left, right or straight through the middle. We weren't sure where the hut was, even though we now know that if it had been daylight we'd have been able to see the red hut quite easily from there. In the darkness, though, its location was anyone's guess. As we sat there contemplating which way to go, we agreed that this would be a New Year's Eve to remember!

Turning off our head torches for a moment, we noticed the tiniest speck of light far in the distance. It was so small and dim, it disappeared when I looked directly at it.

For a minute we thought it might be the light from the hut, but then a second tiny speck of light appeared. They had to be head torches belonging to climbers on the other side of the huge dish. After studying the tiny specks of light appearing and disappearing, moving across the snow, we concluded they belonged to a climbing team making a summit attempt as, at this time of year, these were started at midnight.

Now confident of the hut's position, we seized the moment to take in our surroundings. It was a beautiful night with a clear sky, and no wind at all. The air was warm and inviting even though we were surrounded by snow. We chatted to each other in the silence of the night, our spirits alight with excitement as we rested our weary feet. We knew we were going to make it to the hut, whether it was in the darkness or the light. We were in this together and were almost at the hut, however long 'almost' was.

We set off in the direction of where we'd first seen the specks of light. As we wound back and forth to avoid crevasses, we saw an outrageously big, yellow circle rising over the mountains. Surely this couldn't be the moon? Something had to be playing a trick on our eyes – this bright body looked about the same size as the mountain that it was half-hidden behind. Before our eyes, the moon rose in the sky, shrinking as it went to the regular size we knew it as.

We paused, taking in the stunning scenery revealed by the light of the moon, then we let out a cheer of delight as we spotted a bulky silhouette perched on a far ridge – it was the hut!

Even though our destination was in sight, it was important not to take our eyes off the ball as this is when accidents are likely to happen. Crossing the giant, crevasse-riddled dish kept our minds alert and on task. There's nothing like imagining falling down a crevasse and slowly dying wedged a hundred metres below the surface to keep you awake!

After one last uphill push, we made it to the 33-bunk hut, which sits on the edge of Grand Plateau, 1800 metres above sea level. It was 3.30 am, and we'd been climbing for 22½ hours. Although we were celebrating on the inside, we quietly slipped onto spare bunks to get some shut-eye for the night's few remaining hours of darkness.

We woke to the hum of the other climbers chatting over freshly brewed teas and coffees. Eager for information, we were soon out of our bunks to join them. We found out that, despite being in the thick of the climbing season, no one had summited for the last four days. The warm weather had enticed the crevasses on the upper mountain to open further, potentially beyond the point of being able to be passed. On top of this, the avalanche threat was high.

Doc had radioed the prior night to see if we had arrived safely as not many people start from the bottom. In fact, out of the 20 or so other climbers at the hut, not a single other person there had walked in; instead, they had been helicoptered in.

We listened for the weather report to come through on the radio, hoping for a cold front so we could make our summit attempt that night. The report crackled across the radio mid-morning. There would be no change in the warm weather. This sent the climbing teams in the hut into a frenzy of discussion about what their next moves would be.

Amber and I decided it was not safe to make our summit attempt that night. It would be good to have a rest day in any case, as it would give our bruised feet and stiff limbs time to recover and we would be able to drink plenty of water to properly rehydrate.

As it was still early enough in the climbing season, we hoped the weather would change and freeze over. We spent the day assessing the view of the upper half of the mountain and discussing the finer details of the route we planned to take. We studied our map until we were happy that we were ready for our summit attempt. Then, once all our preparation and planning was complete, we cracked open a small bottle of bubbles each. We had carted these up the mountain in our packs to say cheers to the New Year!

The next morning, we waited for the weather report with our fingers crossed, even though the weather outside the window had lowered our hopes.

We had spent a lot of time preparing for this adventure, taken time off work and saved up to pay for what was not a cheap expedition. For a second, I felt like that would all go to waste if we didn't summit — but that was far from the case! We'd already had one hell of a fun adventure and learnt some invaluable lessons about the mountain and ourselves.

The room hushed as the radio crackled once more and the weather report came through. Our hearts sank when we heard there was still no change in the forecast and that there wouldn't be for the next few days. The forecast wasn't terrible, but the warm weather meant an increase in avalanche risk, ice bridges melting and collapsing, and crevasses opening up at an alarming rate.

For climbers, the weather can be tricky to assess as the forecasts aren't always accurate. If the weather is either really good or really bad, decisions are easier to make, but when the weather is not ideal, but not terrible, you really have to evaluate the pros and the cons.

Amber and I had a long discussion about our next move. Given we'd come so far, should we just go for the summit despite the weather conditions? We overheard other teams who'd decided to make the attempt. Should we follow suit? Should we organise more time off work so we could wait at the hut for a few more days? Should we just finish our adventure and head home?

Even though we had compelling arguments for each option, deep down we both knew the decision had already been made. Without a safe enough weather window to make a summit attempt, it was time to head home. We weren't disappointed by not having summited; instead, we were excited by the adventure we'd just had. We felt proud to have climbed the first half of the great Mount Cook, and we were determined to return to climb to the summit one day.

DON'T BE AFRAID TO FAIL

One thing I cannot stress enough is the importance of being smart in your decision-making and not being blinded by wanting to conquer or complete a challenge. Being determined and having the fire in your belly to push through all barriers on an adventure or challenge is important but, even more important, is knowing when to call it and walk away. Not being able to recognise the time to stop can be detrimental in any situation. To go into an adventure with the blind attitude of 'I must conquer this challenge no matter what' is how people can get themselves into serious trouble.

We get one life – and that life is for living, adventuring, exploring, having fun and challenging yourself, but *not* at all costs. We can make attempts and learn from them. If they don't pan out, we can always try again until we succeed.

Some people believe turning around would be 'failing', so they are not prepared to do so. They feel too ashamed to turn around or pull the pin, which is a detrimental way to approach an adventure. The reality is, turning back is not failing – coming home safely and in one piece is always a win!

We should never be afraid to 'fail' as it means you've attempted something in the first place. It means you took that first step, challenged yourself, learnt valuable lessons and will be better equipped to try again in the future.

Some people are so afraid of failing that they won't attempt things in the first place. That is no way to live a fulfilling life. Failure is a natural part of trying and should be seen as a positive thing. We can't expect to achieve everything on the first go, because if we did, how would we ever learn?

Some of the people who are the best at what they do in the world, whether it be adventuring, sports or business, are often the same people who have failed many times. Despite these failures, they have persisted, learning along the way and not getting discouraged. Instead, they have drawn from their experiences in order to achieve their goals.

For us, we knew the mountain would still be there when we were ready for a second or third attempt – when the conditions and circumstances allowed it. That turned out to be in 2017, when we returned and reached the summit. That climb was not without exciting hurdles and even involved us sleeping under a rock for a night, but that is an adventure story for another day!

OPPORTUNITY KNOCKS

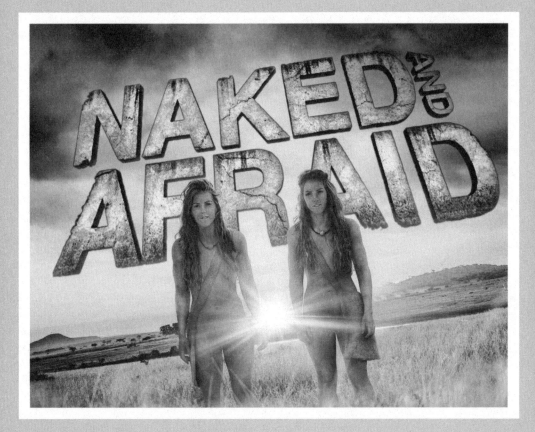

Chapter 11

Opportunity Knocks

South Africa

SERENA

After a sleepless night, we were wide awake in the early hours after dawn. One of the many things that had kept us up were the circling hyenas, which we managed to deter this time. Now with the immediate threat decreased, we joked about how on earth we ended up here.

The opportunity had we seized all started when we were contacted by the crew of the American reality TV series *Naked and Afraid*.

They had found us through social media, where we share our adventures. When they asked if we were interested in doing a *Naked and Afraid* challenge, at first we thought it was someone having a laugh, plus the 'naked' part made us think it couldn't be a real show. We soon got a reply reassuring us they were from a real production company and asking us to consider the challenge as they believed we had the necessary skills to be on the show. This got us thinking.

When we looked into their proposal a little closer, we realised it was all legitimate and found that *Naked and Afraid* airs worldwide on the Discovery Channel. When we were approached to be on it, the show was going into its eleventh series. We watched a few episodes to get a feel for the show. Each episode features two people being dropped into the wilderness where they had to survive for 21 days – completely naked with just one primitive item each. The contestants all had their fair share of challenges and could tap out if things got too much. Some contestants lasted only a few hours on their first day, while others made it through a few days, and others completed the full 21 days.

After seeing the show, we realised that there was nothing distasteful about the 'naked' part. Instead, it was all about survival, and having no clothes was a serious part of the challenge. Had it been the same show with clothes, I don't think it would have been anywhere near as much of a challenge.

We began to consider going on the show and we tossed up the pros and cons. On one hand, this was the ultimate survival challenge, a true test to see if we had what it took to survive in the African wilderness with nothing! When else could we experience that? On the other hand, being naked on TV was a big step for a couple of Kiwis who weren't used to getting their kit off. Despite the cons, we couldn't help but think this was a huge opportunity. No New Zealander had been on the show before, so we would have the chance to show the world how Kiwis do it.

Nervous but excited, we agreed to do the show. Once we'd passed all the mental and physical tests the show's physicians set for us, it was all go. We had only a couple of weeks before leaving New Zealand. This was going to be one hell of a survival challenge. Not having clothes would take our survival skills to their limits, and we wondered whether surviving for three weeks in the African wilderness was even going to be possible.

It was June in New Zealand, so we were heading into winter. Wrapped up in our warm clothes, it was hardly the time to be outdoors doing things like toughening up our feet, ready for the wilderness. However, as soon as we knew we were going to be on the show, we had to prepare and spent the rest of our time walking around barefoot. It wasn't a good start to our survival challenge when I got chilblains on the toes of my left foot, and we hadn't even left New Zealand yet. Amber thought it was hilarious but I struggled to see the funny side of this pain!

The *Naked And Afraid* crew hadn't given us any information about the location of our challenge. We knew we were going to Africa, but Africa is a big place, so we were excited to find out which country we would be spending our time in. About a week before we left, we found out that we would be heading to South Africa. While we were both busy organising a month off work, we jammed in learning as much information on South African as we could.

First, we researched the seasons and weather in South Africa. Naïvely, we thought that being in Africa at least it would be warm. To our despair, we found out that it would be winter in South Africa. In fact, the temperature there would be similar to what we were experiencing in New Zealand. The average temperature was around 4°C overnight. We thought that this couldn't possibly be right. Here, in New Zealand, we were in our winter woollies with our fires lit. No one could survive overnight naked in this temperature, could they?

New Zealand's winters are very wet and can also be quite windy; whereas in South Africa, winter is a dry season and not usually windy. We decided that although the temperatures were similar, New Zealand's wet winter meant it felt a lot colder … surely. *Naked and Afraid* couldn't put us into an environment where it was impossible to survive – could they? We pondered this. We had signed all the usual waivers releasing them of any liability if something were to happen.

We didn't get too hung up on the weather situation; instead, we spent time researching the trees, plants, wood, animals and insects we'd be likely to find in South Africa. We also found out about things we could eat and poisonous things to keep away from. We researched just as much on the things that could kill us as the things that would keep us alive. We pondered and planned what we would do if we were hunted by a lion or hyena, and we talked about what to do if we were confronted by an elephant or rhino.

We brushed up on our fire-starting skills using a primitive hand-drill technique that uses nothing but wood. Once we were confident we could make fire by rubbing wood together, we refreshed and practised starting a fire by using a flint too. Both these techniques can be quite difficult in New Zealand's wet winters as the dead wood in the bush can be waterlogged. However, it works well with materials that are totally dry.

We would have liked more time to brush up on all of this, but soon it was time to go. We were confident enough that our common sense and problem-solving abilities would help us get through any situation. The only part of this survival challenge we were unsure about was the naked bit and how we could survive three weeks out in the elements without the protection of clothes. There was only one way to find out. After all, there's nothing like getting thrown into the deep end to truly find out whether you have what it takes!

After flying for 34 hours, we arrived in the South African province of Limpopo. We were then driven for several hours to a small, remote village, which consisted of a few basic buildings. From the village, we went another 5 kilometres down a dirt road to the little homestead where we'd be staying until we were dropped into the wilderness. The homestead was simple and had a traditional South African hunting vibe with animal skulls lined around the railings of its small outdoor area. Power came from a generator, and the base was one small building, which had everything needed for simple living. While there, we stayed in glamping tents about 50 metres from the house. The place was very remote, and the most exciting part of it was a water hole a hundred metres away from us where we could watch the wild animals come in.

By the time we arrived, it was late at night. We were 10 hours behind New Zealand, so jetlag was in full effect. My eyelids felt as heavy as lead and I couldn't wait a minute longer to hit the hay. Even though we should have been dead to the world in our camp beds, both Amber and I were woken several times throughout the night by cackling hyenas, which sounded like they were just outside our tent. In the distance, we also heard the massive roars of two male lions challenging each other from their neighbouring territories. As well as the ones we recognised, there were all sorts of other noises: roaring, screeching, yelping and grunting.

The following day, we asked the homestead owner which animals might have made the sounds so we knew what dangers were going to be around us. We soon found out that nearly every type of dangerous African animal you could think of was out there, so we would have to sleep with one eye open!

We spent the rest of that day being interviewed about going into the challenge. It was also time to find out which primitive survival items we'd be allowed to take with us into the wilderness. The producers of the show had told us to bring two each, and they would choose one of them for each of us. Between us, we'd brought a machete, a bow with three arrows, some cordage and a mosquito net, which we planned to use as a fishing net if it was chosen.

Jackpot! The producers chose the bow and arrows for Amber and the machete for me. Amber and I both let out a sigh of relief as they couldn't have chosen better. Our machete had a thick, solid blade, which was about 600 mm long, and a strong, wooden, fat-gripped handle with a short loop of cord that I could wrap around my wrist so I didn't accidently let go of it mid-strike. The machete would be invaluable for chopping branches for building our boma, and for protection. A boma is a type of African shelter constructed from thorny branches and sticks. It's usually a head-height enclosure that looks like a giant bird's nest, and it provides a spiky barricade designed to give protection against wild animals.

Meanwhile, having the bow and arrows meant we would be able to hunt, which we were stoked about. The bow was a traditional recurve one, which is basically a string joined to a curved handle. It has no mechanical parts and no sights. It can take a bit of time to master and, although there is a technique to it, you also have to rely on instinct with this type of bow. During our survival testing in New Zealand, we'd proved we were competent with a recurve bow. To back up our skills, we may also have alluded to the fact we'd both been using a recurve for years, when, in reality, we'd only just learnt to use one properly when we found out we were going to be on the show. We learnt as best we could during the few weeks we had to prepare for the challenge. During that time, we figured out our ideal ranges against animal size so we could judge a fatal strike. This last-minute training was less than ideal, but we were confident we could do it as well as anyone else, so it was a case of 'fake it till you make it'.

The producers gave us some zebra hide to do some last-minute decorating on the handle. We wrapped the handle in the hide without much thought. It was only in hindsight, after a few shots, that we found this slight change in handle placement made quite a difference to the balance of the bow.

On our last evening before setting off for the first day of our challenge, we kept warm by sitting around the outdoor fire while wearing warm gear. For a long while, we watched a rhino with its baby and later an elephant come to the water hole for a drink. They were both bigger than we'd imagined – they were similar in size to a truck – and their cautious behaviour silenced us.

We watched and studied their behaviour as the homestead owner explained what they were doing. He told us that when an elephant puffed out its ears then stood side on, it was a warning to us to keep away. Both the rhino and elephant seemed harmless from a distance, particularly with the protection of the building plus the rifles carried by the workers at the homestead. However, we both knew that meeting a rhino or elephant in the wilderness would be a very different story.

The homestead owner cooked a dinner of traditional South African sausage over the fire and the aroma made my mouth water. We sat and ate with him and a few of his staff. The homestead owner was a big, burly man in his early fifties and his family had been on the land for generations. He was a well-known hunter and had a big reputation in the area for being one of the toughest. He could tell you anything you needed to know about the land, although he was unable to divulge many details to us before the challenge.

As we chatted, he told us in a friendly manner that he didn't think it would be possible for someone to survive in this land without clothes or shoes. As I sat next to the fire while wearing a big jacket, I had serious doubts about whether we'd survive the cold too! What also concerned the homestead owner was the fact we wouldn't have shoes to protect us from the thorns. We hadn't thought too much about this until now: in lots of places in New Zealand, you could walk around in the grass and avoid the odd thistle or blackberry thorn and be fine. South Africa was going to be totally different.

He went onto explain that as it was winter, there would be no fruit, edible roots or foliage, and even things like insects, scorpions and snakes would be hibernating so would be very rare. I don't think the production crew had even realised this. It was clear that finding food was going to be extremely difficult for us. He wondered out loud how we could possibly survive without any source of food except for hunting with a recurve bow. He chuckled and said that they could have at least given us a rifle so we had a fighting chance. He also joked that he would probably see us again soon when we tapped out on the first night.

Amber and I don't scare easily, but we were both a little concerned about whether this challenge was going to be possible with the cold, the predators and the lack of food. Before we came to South Africa, we'd studied what types of trees would be in the general area and which trees and plants would be in fruit. Admittedly, we hadn't found many resources for winter time, but according to our research there were going to be a few options when it came to edible fruit and trees.

With a hearty chuckle, the homestead owner said he thought we were either stupider or braver than he was, as we were going into the wilderness without even a rifle. We laughed, hoping it was the latter, and that we would not be back before the 21 days were out. Then he said, 'At least you won't get any rain … It hasn't rained in dry season for more than five years, so I wouldn't bother wasting energy on building a roof.'

We made a mental note of this as it was one thing that would be on our side. The cold was going to be hard enough to survive but cold and wet – no thanks. We were grateful for his reassurance. Although, trust me when I say that anything is possible in the South African wilderness!

NOT CARING WHAT OTHERS THINK

Each time we try something new, we discover things about ourselves and create memories and moments we draw from in the future. These are the things that spark our spirit, our curiosity, empowering us and moulding us into the people we are. However, some people don't want to give things a go because they're worried about failing or embarrassing themselves in front of other people. They care about other people's opinions so much it prevents them from trying new things.

We need to break away from caring about other people's opinions so we can live our lives with ambition and confidence. So what if we embarrass ourselves? So what if we fail? They're both normal parts of life. It's much worse to live with the regret of never having tried things in the first place than to be embarrassed or to fail.

If you're too scared to give things a go, it can hold back your development and the fulfilment you get out of life. This is especially the case with young people who are still trying to find their feet in the world.

If we do embarrass ourselves, is it really that bad, especially when compared to all the benefits we get from giving something new a go? We should live for ourselves instead of letting other people's opinions shape how we live.

The more we jump at new experiences, the more our confidence grows. The more confidence we have, the more we are able to strive for new goals. Having confidence doesn't mean going into an experience thinking you are going ace it. Instead, it means having certainty that no matter what happens, it's all good.

Confidence is not something you either have or don't have. It's something that can be built up over time. The more you do something, the more confidence you will build. One tactic for building confidence can be faking your confidence at the beginning. It won't take long before you no longer need to fake it.

I understand it can be difficult not to take other people's opinions or negative comments on board, especially in today's digital world with keyboard warriors writing things they would never say to a person in real life – often to people they don't even know.

For anyone who struggles with what people might say, a quote that I think is absolutely bang on is this: 'Don't take criticism from someone you wouldn't take advice from.' It is just so true! You would never take advice from that keyboard warrior who knows nothing about your life, so why would you give their criticism a second thought? I know this is easier said than done, but if you remember this quote, it will help you to not focus on negative comments but, instead, to treat it like water off a duck's back. Spread those wings!

INTO THE
WILDERNESS

Chapter 12

Into the Wilderness

South Africa

SERENA

The sun had just broken over the horizon. There was a crispness to the morning's breeze, which made us eager for the sun to rise and warm us because, soon, we would be removing our cosy jackets. For the past hour and a half, Amber and I had been blindfolded while we were being driven further into the South African wilderness.

When the vehicle we were travelling in stopped, we planted our feet firmly on the hard dirt, then our blindfolds were removed. I drew in a few deep breaths to shake off the lingering feeling of car sickness from the very bumpy ground we had travelled across while not being able to see. A shiver ran through me, and I couldn't tell if it was from the cold or my excitement at the adventure ahead.

We swivelled around 360 degrees in an attempt to get our bearings. All I could see was dusty brown earth with dry scrub scattered around it, like the dots on a leopard. In between the scrub, pale brown grasses covered the ground. The scrub was made up of leafless sticks and branches with scarce patches of green foliage. In every direction we looked, the land appeared dry and barren.

On first impressions, it looked like there would be no water for miles. There were a few small, pebble-like droppings on the undisturbed ground and, although these animal droppings were slightly old and stale, there was still a hint of their musky smell in the dry air. Amber and I looked at each other and I could tell we were thinking the same thing – the droppings meant there had to be water somewhere nearby, as the animals needed water to survive.

We orientated ourselves to north and south using the sun, and we noted a few rock formations in the distance, which – along with a couple of taller trees – we would use as landmarks. In order to get going into the African wilderness, we hurried through our filming duties for the morning. This involved the crew interviewing us about how we were feeling now we were minutes away from starting the challenge. The film crew was made up of a team of six, who would be following us around during daylight hours for the duration of the challenge.

In order for the program to be as authentic as possible, once we set off, the film crew were not allowed to talk to or interact with us at all for 21 days – if we could last that long. The lead producer was a woman in her early thirties with a very warm and friendly personality. The camera operators, their assistants and the audio operators were all male. They had all filmed multiple challenges for the show before, so they were all very respectful and professional. We felt comfortable and assured with the team we had.

We knew that Day 1 would be one of the biggest days. Not only did we need to find water, but, to survive our first night, it was vital we were able to gather a good stash of firewood, start a fire and build a boma. If we weren't able to get all of these done before dark, our chances of surviving the night among the lions, hyenas and leopards would be very slim.

On the morning of 22 June, we set off into the African wilderness. The freshness of early morning was disappearing and the sun was just beginning to warm up as we stripped off our clothes next to the vehicle that had dropped us off at our insertion point. Soon, we were completely stark naked. We had pondered how being naked would affect our ability to survive. We'd decided it could even be the single most difficult element of the challenge, even more difficult than dealing with rhinos, leopards and lions.

But for now, at the beginning, being modest people by nature, stripping off in front of a camera crew felt rather strange and hilarious. Amber and I both found it pretty funny, and we chuckled as we thought, 'How the hell did we get here!?' We walked away from our pile of discarded clothes and into the wilderness.

*

Before long, we found two satchels hanging in a nearby tree. They contained a basic map, a pot, flint, my machete and Amber's bow and arrows. As we set off, as naked as the day we were born, within our first few steps we realised we were in for one hell of a ride! Our bare feet made progress across the terrain painfully slowly. Amber and I had to stop every few paces to scrape all the thorns, spiky seeds and prickles from our feet. I think our record was five consecutive steps before stopping to pull out thorns.

There were devil's thorns, which looked like harmless little furry balls. These put a bunch of prickles in your foot, which were painful but easy to get out. Then there were the thorns we called 'nasty buggers'. They were impossible to see but painfully abundant. They had barbs that made them difficult to remove. Lastly, there were the thorns we named the 'bone stabbers'. These weren't as common as they fell only from a few different species of acacia trees, but they were by far the worst! They were long, skinny thorns, which would go so deep into our feet – it felt as if they'd hit bone. They made our feet bleed as they managed to bury themselves deep in our flesh, aggravating us with every step. Worse than that, they continued to make their presence known for a good few days.

Attempting to avoid the thorns, we tried steering clear of a grass we identified as having thorn-like seeds designed to embed themselves into passers-by so they could be carried off to spread. We tried to stick to walking on the bare dirt, and also to avoid the areas around trees that dropped thorns, but nothing we tried made any difference! It didn't seem to matter where we walked – the thorns were everywhere. At the same time, we were on the lookout for the deadly scorpions and snakes, which we knew were commonly found in the area.

By the time the sun was at full height, I started to regret my wish for the warm sun, as the heat made my mouth dry with thirst. The lifeless-looking trees provided very little cover as we walked, and the sizzling sun was out to get us. The basic map we'd found in my satchel showed a water hole quite some distance away, so that was where we were headed.

I found it unbelievable how natural it felt to be naked in the wilderness with no one else around, except the camera crew, who were so professional it almost felt as if they weren't even there. We are not the kind of people I ever thought would be comfortable walking around naked. But there are always things to learn when you get out of your comfort zone; maybe our view on nakedness was about to change – after all, everyone has the same parts!

Just minutes into the challenge, we were no longer worried by our nakedness. The thing that put it to the back of our thoughts was the fact we had much bigger issues to address – like surviving.

As we walked, we studied the terrain, keeping a lookout for anything that might help us later on. I noticed a short, thin piece of wood, which would be ideal to use as our fireboard when it came time to start our fire. I picked it up and stashed it in my satchel. Later, we saw some old elephant dung mounded up on the ground. It was totally hard and dry, the perfect tinder to start a fire. Amber grabbed a good handful and put it in her satchel.

After a few hours walking in the direction of the water hole indicated on the map, we saw some taller trees and greener scrub in the distance. We headed towards them as we knew there must be water there for the trees to grow tall and thicker. We also listened out for birds as this would be a giveaway to lead us to water too.

By early afternoon, we had been covering the harsh terrain for six hours. Our progress had been slow, even though we moved as quickly as we could between the little areas of shade. In the shade, the cold breeze brought goose bumps to my skin. At the same time, being in the direct sun felt like it would not take long to get sunburnt. It was a lose–lose situation. Sunburn would make everything difficult, so it wasn't something we could afford on the first day of our extreme survival challenge.

As I chewed on a piece of grass to keep saliva in my mouth, I realised that thirst had begun to consume me more and more. I could understand how someone might become overwhelmed by panic in a situation like this. We had absolutely no safe haven and no promise that there would be water to drink for who knows how long. I quickly began to realise how vulnerable humans can be. Three days without water is as long as humans can last, but this can be shortened by heat or having to do strenuous tasks. On one episode of *Naked and Afraid*, I had watched a survivalist tap out at the end of Day 1, and now I could understand fully how tempting this might be.

I tried not to think about how much we needed water, but that was a difficult task when all I wanted to do was scull ice-cold water. Amber and I adopted our good old, faithful,

Kiwi attitude, which seems to pull us through every time: 'She'll be right!'

We had each other to keep our spirits high – or high-ish considering our circumstances – and we knew we would just have to deal with it until we found water. Our competitive streak would not let us entertain the thought of tapping out at this early stage.

When we finally reached the trees we'd seen in the distance, we found they were sparse and spread out with one tree to every 5 square metres or so. Some of them had green leaves as small as my thumbnail and others were barren and stick-like, with only long, white thorns. The bird life was humming and their sweet song filled the air. We knew, with this sort of bird life, there had to be water close.

Just 200 metres into the trees, we found a body of water. In our dehydrated state, our spirits soared. The water hole was a misshapen circle, grey-brown in colour with cracked mud crusted around the edges. The water had the consistency of soup. In normal circumstances, no one would dream of drinking from it, but with thirst eating into us and no other water in sight, it wasn't looking half bad.

The water hole was about 30 metres long and 20 metres across at its narrowest point. There was a 3-metre vertical dirt bank on one side, which was scattered with scrub and small trees. Elephant dung floated on the water's edge, not making the slightest bit of difference to the sludgy, dirt-coloured water.

Looking up at the height and angle of the sun, I knew we only had a couple hours of daylight left. Then we'd have another hour of dusk before it would be completely dark and we would be at the mercy of the elements and the wild animals. Despite being very conscious of time, we took a few moments to study the area and pick the best spot to build our boma.

The first night was going to test us, we were sure of that much. Our boma needed to be under cover far enough away from the water source that our presence wouldn't hinder our hunting efforts in the days to come. We studied the ground and the game trails leading to the water hole and took into account wind direction to make sure our scent wouldn't alarm animals and stop them from coming for a drink. We still needed to be close to the water hole as we would need access to the water regularly.

We chose a spot among some thorn-ridden trees on slightly higher ground about a hundred metres away from the water hole. The trees in this spot ranged from 1 to 4 metres high and provided a little natural cover. This meant some of our boma foundation was already built, which gave us the little head start we were in desperate need of, as the sun slowly lowered.

Amber got out the dry, crusty elephant dung and broke it up, ready to use as tinder to get a spark to catch and then walked down to the water hole to collect the water we were very eager to boil. She waded out past the ankle-deep, scummy shallows to try to reach some clearer, undisturbed water. Unfortunately, the deepest it got was about up to her knees, and the water clarity there was not very different to the shallows. Our pot would only hold about two litres of water, which wasn't enough for two well-dehydrated people. Even so, Amber scooped up a potful of this brown, sludgy water to bring back and boil.

We created a bird's nest of fine tinder with larger tinder around the outside, and we added slightly bigger twigs and then some thicker wood, ready to start our fire. We took turns striking the flint, but the shower of sparks would go out instantly. As I tried once more, Amber quickly lifted the elephant dung and blew on it as she saw a tiny spark had struck just for a second. This was all we needed and Amber blew on it, encouraging the tiny spark to take. With a woosh, the smouldering spark burst into flame and we were ecstatic with our creation. This fire was going to help keep us safe against predators while also combating the cold. We sat the beginnings of our fire in the middle of what would soon become our boma and stacked it with twigs and forearm-sized pieces of wood. We couldn't help but keep an eager eye on it. As soon as the fire was established enough, we put on our pot of water to boil, which would then mean we could end our thirst. We hoped like hell there would be enough daylight left for us to boil this small potful, drink it, then refill it ready to boil again for the night, before we were confined to our boma by the predators hunting in the darkness.

For now, I hacked at branches with our machete until the sweat poured off me, while Amber dragged the thorny branches to camp to add to our boma – a shoulder-height circle with a bare dirt floor that looked like a giant bird's nest made of twisted and tangled branches and thorns. We plugged every gap in our boma structure that we could find so there was no easy way for a lion or hyena to get in.

We purposefully chopped and snapped down branches from the thorn-ridden trees to give us the best protection against the predators. The thorny branches took a long time to collect, as we had to negotiate the thorns with all our exposed skin then walk the branches back across the thorn-peppered ground to our boma site.

Before the challenge, I'd imagined the cold would be the most difficult aspect of being naked in the wilderness, but I had not foreseen how difficult being naked would make even the simplest of tasks. Throughout our lives, we have bush-bashed, collected firewood and macheted down branches to make shelters plenty of times, and I had always taken clothes and boots for granted.

Here, in the South African wilderness, being naked and barefoot meant jobs like collecting firewood took hours and seemed to never end. Without the protection of clothes, we had to adapt the way we collected wood. We could no longer collect a big armful as it would rip our skin to pieces. Instead, we collected it piece by piece. We had to take the extra time to walk around the scrub as shortcutting through it, like we would have with clothes on, would leave us scratched and grazed.

The wood-gathering process was further slowed by the risk of being caught off guard by deadly scorpions. Having talked to locals and studied scorpions online back home, we felt we had a good chance of determining how venomous particular types were. We knew they typically lived under dead wood that was lying on the ground, which is what we were collecting for firewood. To combat this danger, every time we picked up a piece of wood, we had to throw it back on the ground. This gave the wood a good shake, causing any scorpions to fall out of the cracks.

Progress seemed to happen at a snail's pace, and we knew dusk wasn't far away. We breathed heavily with the effort as we hurried to build our boma as best we could and collected the firewood we needed to last the entire night. After our exhausting day with no food or water yet, I was surprised we still had the energy to work this hard, but fear of being exposed to lions or hyenas in the night spurred us on and we ignored any hints of exhaustion coming from our bodies.

Even though the cold chill of the late afternoon was upon us, we were sticky with sweat as a result of our furious efforts. Our pot had boiled but the water was still far too hot to drink. Without any other way to hold the boiled water while it cooled, we realised there wouldn't be time to get a second pot of water. One small pot between both of us was going to have to be enough to get us through the night.

Things started to get pretty real as dusk began approaching! The camera crew set up trail cameras all around our base and in our boma and were now packing up, ready to leave. It was mandatory for the camera crew to have left before dusk as, even though they had rifles, it was unsafe for them to be out in the open. The creeping dusk brought with it the feeling of vulnerability, so we made a last-ditch effort to grab some big, slow-burning logs for firewood. We couldn't slip up by letting out fire burn down, even for just a moment, as that would be all the predators needed.

The crew had left and, with the sun disappearing, there was nothing further we could do. We grabbed the spiky, door-sized branch we had left beside the entrance to our boma. We walked in through the small gap that was our entrance and plugged it with the big branch so there was no longer any access inside. We were completely surrounded by our nest of spiky branches. Although we enjoyed having time to ourselves with the camera crew no longer on our every move, we felt an eerie stillness as darkness approached. Looking around, we spotted a few gaps here and there in our boma, but we had run out of time, so it would have to do for the night.

As the light faded, leaving us in a shadowy haze, the silence was interrupted by the sound of hooves beating on the firm ground. We peered over the top of our boma and, through the football-sized gaps among the trees, we could just see down to the water hole. Amber and I simultaneously gasped at the sight of antelope of all kinds cautiously coming in to drink water. The impalas, which were similar in size to New Zealand's fallow deer, grunted and snorted on their approach to the water hole, and we watched as about eight of them were brave enough to expose themselves to potential predators by taking a drink.

The impalas were followed by a couple of kudu, which were lanky and goofy-looking, with oversized ears and hooves. One kudu was a huge male, bigger than a horse, and it had two spiralled, curly horns that were a metre long. The second kudu, a female, was followed by its young. They were even more cautious about taking a drink than the impalas. There were bushbucks and duikers too; both are types of antelope. Duikers are one of the smallest of the antelopes and are similar in size to sheep. Then we spotted a zebra inching back and forth as it built up the courage to get to the water. What a sight!

For the moment, we forgot about our thirst, the stinging cuts and scratches all over us and the predators that would be coming with nightfall. Instead, our eyes were alight with wonder at the beautiful animals we were watching. The hardship of the day all seemed worth it in this moment.

During the day, the land had looked so barren that it seemed there would be no animals at all for miles, but now our area was alive with activity. The dry season meant there would be very little water at all nearby, and these animals were no different to us – they needed to quench their thirst badly enough to take the risk of going to the water hole.

Our water pot had cooled just enough for us to take very small sips. We were so desperate for the dryness in our mouths to be relieved, we didn't even worry about the consistency and colour of the water. Although the liquid felt soothing and good on our sticky tongues, we were disappointed it did not quench our thirst. We put it down to the water still being quite hot from the fire and looked forward to when it cooled completely.

As the darkness engulfed us, the animals disappeared from the water hole and we were left in eerie silence broken only by the odd yelping jackal. We were drawn to the warmth of the fire and, as we sat next to it, we whispered to each other. In the silence of the night, our whispering felt like we were shouting, which would give away our position to predators.

Looking around at our defences, we prepped ourselves for the night. We armed ourselves with a branch the same thickness as our forearm, which we carved into spears. In desperation, these could be used to club or stab a snarling head poking through the side of our boma. I also had my machete, which I had placed comfortably next to me so it would be easy to grab when I woke up. Searching around for it in the darkness could cost me precious seconds. Amber did the same with the broad tip of an arrow and her bow was propped ready on a branch of our boma wall.

We examined the walls of our boma as the light from the fire flickered over it. We were horrified to realise that the small gaps we had noticed earlier now looked like gaping holes, which we thought would require little effort for a snarling hyena or stealthy leopard to push through. We could barely believe this boma and the fire were our only defences against a lion, hyena or elephant! But we had to trust these defences – Africans have used these techniques for centuries.

Sitting there in our boma, we wondered what was lurking in the darkness just metres away – we couldn't believe how exposed we had left ourselves. Even so, we knew we couldn't have done anything about it earlier, as we had pushed our bodies as hard as possible before we ran out of time.

It didn't take long to notice how incredibly hard the ground was on our bare skin. The ground was plain old dirt and not the spongy type either. It was hard, dry, dusty, cracked dirt covered with tiny rocks and sharp twigs, which made it difficult to sit still or lie down.

It was hard to be sure of the time or how long it had been dark, and there was no moon to reference off, but we guessed it was two hours into the night when the howling and cackling begun. I threw another piece of wood on the fire as the animal noises grew closer and clearer. I told myself the animals were only getting closer because they were curious and wanted to check out this strange thing on their land. But, in truth, I knew hyenas worked in packs and were real opportunists. If they saw any opportunity for a kill, they would not hesitate to lunge at it. Working in a pack, they would be well beyond difficult to fight off. The hyenas were much bigger than I'd imagined, with the top of their backs standing halfway up my waist. As well as the hyenas, we could hear the growl of a leopard or perhaps a lion, off in the distance.

Not only were we stoking the fire for protection against animals, but also to fight against the cold. It was freezing! Ever since I'd cooled down from my earlier efforts, I had been trying to bite down to stop my teeth from clattering as I shivered. Our fire was not enough to keep this much exposed skin warm. I nudged forwards, closer and closer, until I was so close to the fire it felt as though my skin was burning, but I didn't care as long as I got as much heat as possible.

On that first night, I thought about some of the small things I hadn't previously considered, which gave me a true appreciation for the life I lead. I sat on the hard ground, among the dirt and twigs, and I had to adjust my position every few minutes to prevent my bottom from aching or my legs from going dead. There was no way to get comfortable without clothing providing a barrier against the gravel-like ground.

As the night went on, we lay down, curled around the fire to get as much heat as we could. Still, my shivering went on as the side of my body that was facing away from the fire took the brunt of the cold. I had to adjust my position every few minutes as stones and sharp twigs dug into my bare flesh.

I soon realised we wouldn't have to worry about falling asleep for too long and not waking up to stoke the fire. It felt like I was waking every five minutes as a result of either the noises outside the boma, the cold or my dead and aching hips and shoulders from lying on the hard dirt. When the fire burnt down even slightly, eager for warmth, one of us would stoke it too much so we then had to shuffle back fast to avoid getting burnt.

During the night, the water in our pot had cooled, so Amber sat up and lifted it to her lips for a much-anticipated scull. She spluttered and only managed a gulp. I followed and I too had the same reaction. The water tasted salty, and we could only manage a gulp at a time despite our extreme dehydration. It didn't make sense. When the water hit my dry mouth, it felt amazing, but as soon as I swallowed it, I found the salty flavour left my mouth dry and unsatisfied. 'Surely it can't be salt water?' I said to Amber. 'It must just be the dirt or minerals.'

To keep our minds off what lurked in the darkness, we talked quietly through the rest of the night, planning to get big, spiky branches to close the gaps and weak points in our boma. We plotted how we would collect a huge amount of green foliage to plug all the tiny holes to stop the wind whipping through. We planned to collect the sandy dirt we had seen kicked up by animal hooves and cart it to our boma to sleep on. And we discussed where we would build our blind so we could start hunting.

The sun rose and Day 2 was about to begin. Our heavy eyes and the tiredness caused by the sleepless night seemed to disappear with the darkness. We waited until it was fully light before we pushed out the spiky branch that was our door. Even though it felt too cold to leave the fire this early in the morning, we made a dash to get another pot of water. With no food, we didn't have the time-consuming task of cooking or eating, and we soon realised how much of our time back at home revolved around food.

We had made it through the first night and optimistically thought that if we'd managed to do that, we could make plenty more. We would later find that the wilderness had many more challenges ahead.

GET OUT OF YOUR COMFORT ZONE

Getting out of your comfort zone can lead to some of the most meaningful experiences in life, opening you up to achievements you may have thought beyond your capabilities. It's a way to build up your inner strength and confidence, and open doors that may have previously been closed by your own barriers. It can be hard to take that leap away from the safety of routine, but, in my experience, it has always been worth it 10 times over.

Taking this leap enables you to learn new things and grow as a person, which can change the direction of your life. I like the saying, 'Life begins at the end of your comfort zone.' I believe that each time we try something new, we open up the endless possibilities of where this could take us. It can bring to life our creativity and enable us to become more adaptable to change, in this forever-changing world.

Change means you are moving forwards, challenging yourself and discovering new things about yourself. When you try something new, whether you succeed on your first attempt, tenth attempt or not at all, the practice of leaving your comfort zone will have seen you grow and develop. A mind that has grown doesn't go back to its old dimensions.

The more you move outside your comfort zone, the more your fear of the unknown will disappear. That fear will then be replaced by empowerment and achievement.

When you leave your comfort zone and do something new for the first time, you may find you absolutely love it, or you may find it doesn't quite go to plan and you might not enjoy yourself at all. Either way, it's still a good thing as, even if you didn't enjoy yourself, it means you've figured out that it's not something you want to do again and you can stop wondering 'what if?'

THE HUNT

Chapter 13

The Hunt

South Africa

SERENA

One of the most pressing questions facing us was how we would hunt when it took us so long to cover only a small amount of ground. Even with the weeks of toughening our feet before we left home, our bare feet were no match for the dusty, dry, thorn-riddled ground. To cross just 50 metres of ground took us a good few minutes walking in slow motion, trying our best not to step on thorns and stopping to pull them out when they became unbearable.

With so much skin exposed, we couldn't afford to be out in the open in the burning sun for too long. To avoid more scratches and torn skin, we had to walk around trees and scrub instead of bush bashing through it, which would have allowed us to shortcut through gaps in the trees when tracking animals.

Standing barefoot, totally naked in the South African wilderness with nothing but our machete and our bow and three arrows, we knew we were going to have to muster all our skills and cunning to hunt successfully in these conditions, but was that even going to be possible?

We were devastated to discover the homestead owner had been right – the winter season ensured there were no trees in fruit. On top of that, there were also no edible roots in the area, no edible foliage (when we could actually find green foliage) and no insects we could eat to get us through. Our hope of being able to forage native flora to eat faded before our eyes. If we wanted to eat, our only option was going to be to hunt wild game.

We wondered how long we could go without food. Could we last a week? Two? The full 21 days? Amber could barely skip a meal back home, so we concluded we'd manage a couple of days at the most before we needed food.

We would have to adapt to our new environment and quickly learn to hunt in this land, as our survival depended on it. We decided our best bet was going to be to build a blind near the water's edge and let the animals come to us.

On Day 2, we took the time to scope out the immediate area around our water hole and study the animal signs and the direction of their tracks. As we were scrutinising a set of hoof prints, I noticed a fresh set of large leopard footprints. I yelled at Amber to come and take a look.

A chill went down my spine when I realised we hadn't even heard a leopard during the night. Mind you, the homestead owner had given us a warning: 'You're unlikely to see or hear a leopard until it's on top of you with its jaws around your throat and its hind legs kicking to rip your abdomen open.' He had painted a sobering picture.

Even though we were keen to get out of the sun, we wanted to check out the afternoon action at the water hole. In this dry environment, animals would surely come to quench their thirst while the sun was at its hottest. We sat downwind and out of sight behind some scrub at one end of the water hole to see if animals came in at this time.

We chopped and dragged some branches over to our spot to provide us with some more cover. We hadn't been sitting there for long when a warthog ran out of the scrub towards the water hole. Warthogs are funny looking things, and this black, coarse-maned warthog had a great set of tusks! It stopped short of the water and, with its tail straight up in the air, it jumped from side to side as it looked for predators.

It must have decided that things were OK as it soon charged into the water and began slurping up the murky sludge. Then it went in a little deeper to bathe. In the meantime, Amber and I (and probably the film crew) held our breath in excited anticipation. We could hardly believe a warthog had just bowled in out of nowhere. We hadn't expected to hunt from this position, but Amber had the bow and was slowly getting into position. The warthog was about 50 metres away, which was more than double the range of the bow.

Unfortunately, the warthog didn't even come close to being within range before it took off into the scrub after it had heard a suspicious rustling of leaves on the opposite side of the water hole. This encounter made our spirits soar and we were excited to build a blind so we could start hunting.

Hunting is best done at dusk or dawn, and the animal activity we'd witnessed from the safety of our boma at dusk had proved this. Annoyingly, though, it was not an option for us as it was prime time for predators too, and we did not want to risk being hunted. From the roaring we had heard in the night and our close encounters with hyenas, we knew how real that possibility was.

The location of our blind was the key to giving us our best chance of a successful hunt. We chose a tree downwind, close to the water hole, but, unfortunately, it was still quite a distance for a bow shot. We stepped out the distance from the blind to different spots around the water's edge. Knowing how far we needed to shoot would enable us to aim accordingly.

From our blind, the closest point of the water's edge was 20 metres away, so we decided we wouldn't take a shot unless the animal was standing in that spot or closer to us. With our recurve bow, premium range was 10 metres, but up to 20 metres was also within range. A long shot would be about 30 metres, which was possible but tricky, and would likely give the animal time to react to the noise of the twang of the arrow. Anything further than 30 metres would be out of range, so this was going to be a game of close quarters involving stealth and strategy.

The tree we chose for our blind had a few scraggly branches that went right down to ground level and little green leaves dotted through its branches. The cover this tree provided was scarce, but it gave us a base from which to start building our blind. We were more than 24 hours into the challenge, and we'd had no food and were terribly dehydrated. We were already starting to think about conserving energy, so were cautious not to waste any on unnecessary tasks.

We were caught between wanting to build a really good blind or chucking up something as quickly as possible. If we took the first option, which might take several days at our new, conservative pace, we risked tainting the area with human scent, but ultimately we would be well concealed from our prey, giving us a better chance of making a kill. If we took the second option, we'd spread less human scent and we could begin hunting straight away. However, the blind wouldn't camouflage us as well, so our chances of a successful hunt could be slimmer.

After a quick back-and-forth discussion, Amber and I agreed on the quick option, with a compromise that we could still add to the blind each day if we needed to. This would allow us to get into position as fast as possible, so we didn't give away our presence in the area.

We made a good start on our blind, but as the sun started to get low and the evening set in, we retreated to the safety of our boma. That night was cold and miserable. At some ridiculous hour of the morning, probably around 2 am, as we sat by the fire stoking it up for warmth, I looked up in disbelief. I thought I'd felt a few spits of water fall out of the darkness. No way! Surely it couldn't be rain – could it? According to the homestead owner, it never rained in dry season so we'd decided not to bother exerting energy to put a roof on our shelter. The first droplets hissed as they hit our fire, but soon the rain got harder and heavier. My teeth chattered uncontrollably – it was only about 5°C and the rain made it feel even colder. We backed into the corner of our boma, which provided some natural shelter from the tree. The fire was stoked high, but as we sat and watched the rain attack it, we prayed the coal bed would be big enough to stop it from going out completely. We needed the flame both for warmth and to deter predators. We sat in the darkness shivering for what felt like an eternity until the rain eventually eased off.

As the darkness gave way to morning light, the rain stopped altogether. We stoked up the fire and began to thaw out. Amber and I laughed at how naïve we'd been not to build a roof. We knew what we were going to be doing in the day ahead!

After spending the morning making a roof and finishing off our blind, we crept into the blind. We'd hacked down some branches and intertwined them into the tree's branches to create a semi-circular wall to hide behind. We made sure there were a few holes in the blind's wall through which our arrow could poke. Even a tiny green leaf could deflect the arrow enough to prevent the shot from hitting its target.

In the blind, we alternated between sitting and standing in silence. To fill the long hours of waiting and watching, Amber and I talked under our breath. We could only sit on the rock-hard dirt for a few minutes before we had to adjust our numb or sore legs and bottoms.

With human activity at a halt while we hunted, it was peaceful to watch the area come to life as we took in our beautiful surroundings. Small, sparrow-sized birds filled the branches of the surrounding trees, and there would be a loud hum each time they took flight, going back and forth, dancing in the trees. We watched some ground birds that were slightly smaller than pheasants creep out of cover towards the water's edge. Then as quickly as they'd come, they were gone.

A couple of hours into the stillness, we watched a couple of very skittish impalas come in to drink water. They were pretty much at one of the furthest spots on the far side of the water hole, more than 60 metres away. We wondered if they had come in at that position because they had sensed we were here, or if it was just a coincidence that they had entered so far away from us. Either way, it was exciting to watch them slowly become more daring to get to the water for a drink before bolting off. Only one of the impala actually got a drink before it sprang away as if it had been spooked by something in the water, like a crocodile. This spurred the other impala to dart off in a panic before it even got to the water.

Hunting in the blind was our only plausible way to get food, but it meant we were unable to do anything else, and we still had to allocate time to collect and boil water, collect firewood and improve our boma each day.

As it was already late in the afternoon, we decided to leave the blind and do everything else we had made a good start on first thing that morning. There was no way we could let ourselves be caught short on any of those tasks as it would expose us to the wild animals, and we were pretty keen on living to the end of this challenge!

The following morning, we were eager to get back in the blind. It was curious that we weren't hungry. We'd thought we wouldn't make it long without food, but here we were four days in and not actually hungry.

Each morning and evening, the camera crew would drive in, then walk the last couple of kilometres to where we had set up our camp. They tried to be stealthy, but we could tell they hadn't done much hunting before as the noise they made travelled a long way in the stillness of the wilderness.

Sitting in the blind, I pondered how different it would be if it had just been Amber and I without the camera crew. The experience would be similar, as the crew never interacted with us; however, if it had been just Amber and me, we would have been invisible to the animals.

Amber and I kept to the same paths, not only because we'd swept the thorns away, but also so there was less chance of human scent being spread around. By now, we smelled of the land and smoke. We washed in the water hole every so often, but any hint of soap or shampoo was well gone. The wind direction was still in our favour from the blind, so any animals upwind wouldn't be able to detect us.

The camera crew made sure they didn't wear any smelly perfumes or deodorants or use perfumed soaps or shampoos. Even so, our senses were heightened and reset as a result of our simple life, so each day the camera crew arrived, we could often smell their cleanness even before we heard them.

After a couple hours in the shade of the blind, we couldn't take the shivering any longer. We stepped out of the back of the blind slowly to prevent detection. We trod so lightly that our feet made no sound as we moved across the ground.

Still shielded by the blind, we stepped into the sun. The warm sun on our skin felt glorious as we stood there getting warmed through. We couldn't stay out in the sun too long, as we wouldn't be in position if an animal approached the water hole. We stayed in the sun just long enough for the warmth to soak in and make our next stint of shivering in the shade of the blind bearable, then we crept back into the blind with renewed morale and focused attention.

Not long after we got back into the blind, we spotted movement in the shrubs on the far side of the water hole. We caught glimpses of a dark shape going back and forth, then I spotted the warthog's legs as it crossed a hole in the cover of scrub. Even though we were about 80 metres away, we didn't move a muscle in fear it would sense us and run off. Animals certainly aren't dumb – their senses are far superior to a human's. As we had seen in the evenings, the animals were already super cautious without humans added to the mix.

The camera crew's blind was about 100 paces behind us. Although they'd made a good effort not to be spotted, it was not good enough. With building frustration, we watched as the crew moved around, talking quietly, seemingly unaware that their movement would give us away or that there was even an animal nearby. If we could hear and see them, the animals certainly would be able to as well.

We hadn't anticipated how ridiculously hard it would be to hunt with six people following our every move, and we were now very worried the added humans were damaging our chance of getting food. Once the animals realised humans were in the area, they might not take the risk of drinking from this water hole. We desperately signalled to the camera crew to stop, hoping that they would do so before the animal broke out into the open.

The bristle-haired warthog came in on the far side of the water hole. Again, it had entered the area as far away from us as possible and completely out of range for a shot. This was clearly not a coincidence.

The warthog moved away before it even got to the water and our confidence that our hunt would be successful slowly slipped away with it. We were going to be hard pressed to get an animal to come close enough for a shot with the camera crew spooking them.

As the warthog darted out of sight, a terrible squealing pierced the air followed by thumping and the grunts of a struggling animal. We heard a tussle and low growling as the warthog took its last breath. Had it succumbed to the attack of a leopard? Or was it a lion? It had to be one of the two, and we shuddered at the thought.

The hair stood up on my arms when I realised how close the predator must have been. Judging by how soon the squealing started after the warthog left, the predator was too close for comfort. How long had it been there? Had it been stalking us and got distracted by the warthog?

Twice that day, single impalas made it to the water's edge. The first time we heard them grunting but we couldn't quite place the sound. Then we heard faint hooves on the ground as a small group of impalas lingered on the edge of the scrub, the sweet scent of water luring them in. The male impala would grunt and stomp its hooves as if rounding up the group, and the females would slowly come in together. Then one would let out a high-pitched grunt as a warning signal and the group would scatter away in fright. We quickly became familiar with their grunting, which would make our hearts pound with excitement as we waited for them to come into view.

We spent the rest of the afternoon in the blind whispering up a new plan. It was time to change tactics. First, we needed the animals to come in closer and, second, we needed the camera crew to disappear.

I grabbed my machete and chopped down any close thorn-covered branches, then Amber dragged them over to the water hole. We strategically placed the spiky branches all around the water's edge, leaving two large open sections within range of our bow. Our theory was that this would funnel the animals down into the opportune spot, which we had left clear. Surely, they would take the easiest route to get a drink.

Once the camera crew understood the predicament their presence was causing us, they backed off and left their cameras filming from their blinds.

Although the days were long and drawn out, simple tasks like boiling water and sitting in the blind filled our time and the end of each day seemed to come quickly. Each day ended with us scrambling around for firewood.

We spent a bit of time every day picking up thorns until we'd removed the majority of them from our main walking routes. Although this enabled us to move at a quicker pace, we still moved about cautiously as embedded thorns provided us with a painful reminder of their presence with every step. Plus, every now and then, a nearby acacia tree would drop a litter of thorns, so we could never entirely relax.

We retired from our hunting efforts and headed to our boma, a little disappointed with the day's results. Strangely, I felt no hunger at all. I guess my body knew hunger wasn't an option. My stomach felt light with emptiness but totally fine. However, I noticed for the first time that walking had become an effort. We were becoming weaker each day, noticeably losing the spring in our step.

We'd also had upset stomachs for the last couple of days, which added to our weakened state. We boiled our water, so we knew bugs weren't the cause of the problem. We decided the salt in the water was the cause as it was the only thing we'd consumed, and it was getting harder and harder to drink, despite us both being desperate with thirst.

That night, a great thunderous noise in the distance woke us. We could hear whole branches being ripped from trees and the sounds of destruction boomed through the night. Gradually, the noise got closer. Eyes wide with shock, we stoked the fire hurriedly. We watched on, nervously willing the flame from the hot coals to take to the fresh wood.

We could hear trees being plucked out of the ground and thrown down. It sounded like a Tyrannosaurus Rex on the war path. We sat, frozen with terror, praying that whatever it was would head in a different direction.

As the cracking of trees got louder, we could clearly make out the beast breathing as it snorted and chewed. Now, we were in this thing's path! I mouthed the word 'elephant' to

Amber, as no other animal could rag-doll trees as if they were twigs. It was clear the fire wasn't going to deter this beast, so we had to think of something else before it destroyed us too.

We swiftly agreed that noise might deter it, so we stood up and – with adrenaline coursing through us – we began banging a branch on our pot and yelling as loud as we could. The noise rang out into the night with startling intensity.

I wasn't sure whether the racket was attracting or deterring the beast as, apart from a quick pause, it hadn't slowed its approach. The last thing we wanted to do was provoke it further.

When it was just 20 metres from our boma, it finally came to a stop. We could just make out its huge black shadow dwarfing the scrub in front of it. It was enormous!

As our first plan hadn't made much difference, we decided to try plan B. We sank back into our shelter and backed up under our tree. We figured if we were really quiet, it might lose interest in us. Hardly daring to breathe, we listened to it take another few steps. We then heard a snort followed by the soft, muffled thuds of each footprint as it turned away and walked off down to the water hole.

To our dismay, within minutes, we heard the noise of trees being ripped down once again. Even worse than that, it was heading back in our direction. As the great mass came towards us, I began to rethink our greatest risk out here in the wilderness. I had thought it was lions and leopards, but now I wondered if I'd been greatly mistaken. If this elephant decided to charge us, it would be a miracle if we survived.

We stood up, stretching to look out in the direction of the racket. Hearts beating out of our chests, we froze when we saw the elephant heading straight towards us, one thunderous step at a time. It was so close, I could see its skin had dark patches where it had sprayed water on itself, and its huge ears flapped back and forth as it walked towards us. Its golf-ball-sized eyes seemed to be fixed on us, but I couldn't read the mood behind them. It was a lone bull elephant – great, the most dangerous ones.

Almost as if it was toying with us, the elephant stopped and grabbed a branch from a tree only a few metres from our boma, then it flapped its ears back and forth and let out a loud trumpeting sound. It went silent as it drew in a breath through its trunk, tasting the scent of the air.

In the firelight, we didn't dare move. To our horror, it then walked towards our boma. We thought we were goners. I caught Amber's eye as she signalled towards the fire. Slowly, but with confidence, I grabbed a burning log to wave around, while Amber banged on the pot.

A couple of metres away, the elephant hesitated, and I wondered if this was the final moment before it was going to charge. Then it puffed a spray of saliva through its trunk before turning and moving off into the night.

For the next few hours, we sat by the fire, adrenaline still pumping through our bodies. We were worried it might circle around and come back again, but thankfully the elephant left us alone for the rest of the night.

*

Over the next few days, we tried everything possible to replenish our energy. We shaved bark off trees and wove it into ropes, which we used to set snare traps in hope of catching a small ground bird. We trawled through the water hole in case an eel was hiding in the thick mud. We explored the trees for any signs of a bird's nest. We looked for insects and snakes all around. There was nothing – the land was barren.

Our tactic of using thorny branches to block off the sides of the water hole worked exceptionally well. It brought animals down to the spot we had left open on the closest side. Even so, our problem was a lack of animals. We saw one a day if we were lucky.

On one occasion, an impala walked into view and Amber got into position to knock an arrow. The impala stopped several times, threatening to bolt before it got in close enough for Amber to take her shot. Each time, we held our breaths until it took another couple of steps forward.

She drew back the string to let the arrow fly. Time slowed as the string twanged loudly. The arrow flew slightly high, just above the hair on the spine of the impala, and the animal bolted. Bummer! Even though we were disappointed, our spirits were high after actually getting a shot.

We thought it was a little strange that the shots had gone high, after my shot played out identically. Then, eventually, we realised the zebra hide around the hand grip might be altering the angle at which we held the bow, so we got rid of that straight away.

During our afternoon firewood haul on Day 6, we came across a delightful surprise. Amber threw a piece of firewood at the ground to dislodge anything dangerous before she picked it up to take back to the boma. She pointed excitedly at the ground, yelling 'Scorpion! Scorpion!'

There was no way we could allow this scorpion to scurry away, I handed Amber the machete. Keeping my feet well out of the away, I lifted the log and gasped when I saw the scorpion. It was black and hairy with a bulging armoured shell, and it stretched to about 7 centimetres long, with a fat tail about 2 centimetres wide. It had little pincers but a large tail, which I knew held a vicious sting. From our research, we knew small pincers meant the sting on its large tail would likely be deadly.

I yelled, 'Careful!' as the scorpion's venomous tail rippled towards Amber as she closed in on it.

With one hand holding the machete, Amber stabbed the scorpion, cutting its head in half and instantly killing it. Even when scorpions are dead, you have to be extremely careful as their tails can whip up and sting as a reflex. Amber cut off the end three sections of its tail, which held the venom, rendering the rest of the scorpion's body safe. We were sad to see a third of our meal go to waste, but it had to be done.

Back at the boma, our fire was smouldering low as we made sure our hot coals lasted the day. We placed the scorpion on a forked twig and held it over the coals until it was charred and bubbling with heat. It shrivelled to half its size and by the time we cut it in half, we had one small bite each. There was barely any meat on it, just an empty crunchy shell, but even so the flavour was incredible! It tasted like a crunchy crayfish and it didn't need any kind of seasoning to enhance its flavour – it was perfect. We chewed on the shell-like exterior, savouring the flavour. I wondered if it really did taste that good or whether my taste buds were fooling me after so long without food.

With every day that passed, there was less chance of us getting a real meal as the animals became more aware of our presence. By Day 7, our morale was sinking. It had been a full week, and the half mouthful of scorpion had had little effect on our energy levels.

Our funnel tactic on the water's edge was no longer working for the odd animal that still dared to venture in for a drink. The animals were familiar with our presence, so instead of being funnelled down to the water's edge close to us, they risked jumping the thorny barrier so they could get a drink further away.

I started to ponder whether we could actually do the full 21 days with no food, as that was starting to look like the most likely outcome. Although we felt a lot weaker than normal, we felt fine in regards to 'starvation'. Back home, if you'd asked me how long I could go without food, I probably would have said a day, maybe less for Amber. Out here, though, it was different from what I'd imagined. We were on Day 7 with no food and I still didn't feel hungry. The mind is a wonderful and powerful thing. With our subconscious knowing there was no food, no pantry and no supermarket, it did not overwhelm us with hunger.

Although I didn't feel hungry, I was very aware of the changes in our energy levels. We both moved slower and small actions felt laborious. Standing up too fast would leave us lightheaded. Something as effortless as a walk seemed to fatigue us considerably now and we fought the temptation to nap all day.

I could feel how weak my body was becoming so I knew we couldn't give up on hunting. Persistence usually pulls us through, no matter how long it takes. Although Amber and I are very competitive, we are also pretty level-headed, so we knew that if we felt we were at risk of long-term health issues, we would have pulled the pin – health is everything!

On the afternoon of Day 8, we hadn't seen any animals come in the whole day until I heard the unmistakable grunt of an impala. The noise got our blood pumping with excitement every time we heard it, and I slowly rose to my feet in anticipation. I reached out to break off a twig that was obscuring my vision when Amber stopped me with a hiss as a lone impala buck came into view. At this stage, every move we made was make or break, as the animals had become ridiculously skittish.

I focused on getting into position and knocking my arrow while Amber's eyes were glued on the impala. Not even daring to whisper, we started our ritual to get in shooting stance. Amber remained seated while I was on my feet. She grabbed my ankle. Every squeeze of my ankle meant 'freeze' or 'go'. It was like a very serious game of statues!

Each time the impala showed the slightest hesitation, even if it blinked in our direction, Amber halted me so it wouldn't detect us. I reacted to every ankle squeeze with slow, subtle movements.

This was a good-sized buck with impressive, dark, curled horns, about half a metre long. The impala was still inching towards the water's edge. I let out an internal sigh of disappointment as I watched it jump the barrier of thorns instead of coming closer to us to get to the water's edge. My heart pounded hard, and the thumping sounded as if it was in my ears.

I had the arrow knocked and my arm muscles strained as I pulled the string back fully extended. The impala was past the barrier of branches and there was only a metre to go before it got to the water's edge. It had to be more than 35 metres away, but we were past desperate. I had to give it a crack as we might not get another chance.

Amber whispered, 'Hold it … hold it …'

My arm had started to shake with the strain, and I could feel droplets of sweat appearing on my brow. I was surprised I could pull back the rigid string at all, given how weak I was feeling, but adrenaline pulsed through my veins and took over my body.

The impala had made it to the water's edge and, although it still threatened to bolt with every twitch of movement, it lowered its head to take a drink.

I released my grip and let the arrow fly.

The arrow flickered through the air, too fast for our eyes to follow. Then I heard a thud and I saw the strike. It was a hit! I had never seen a sight so spectacular. While I took no pleasure in the distress of this magnificent animal, I believe in harvesting what the land provides; it's the circle of life.

The impala's legs gave way a little as bright red blood spurted out, but then it straightened and spun around 180 degrees before bolting off, with the arrow doing more damage as it ran. It had been a long shot for a recurve bow, so the impala had had the slightest time to spook and jump at the twang of letting go of the string a split second before the arrow landed. The arrow had landed a little further behind its front shoulder than I would have liked, but I had my fingers crossed it would still do the job. It had to be sheer adrenaline that spurred on the impala as it sprang out of sight.

Amber and I looked at each other with shocked expressions. We were both stunned by the shot, as we had thought it was too far-fetched. Our persistence, spending painstaking hours upon hours in the blind even when we thought it was pointless, had finally paid off.

We jumped up in excitement and talked over the details of my shot. We walked over to the edge of the water hole. As we looked down at the dusty ground, we saw the blood trail the impala had left behind. The fact it was losing blood meant it would be less difficult to track and made us hope it would be down in no time. After all, our battered, thorn-stricken feet meant we weren't up for a chase, especially in our weakened state.

We were about a hundred metres away from the water hole, still following the blood trail, when some huge prints stopped us dead in our tracks. These tracks were pretty fresh and they didn't belong to an elephant. The only other thing as big as an elephant was a rhinoceros.

We stopped for a minute. We'd been so excited by the hunt that we'd let our usual vigilance slip. Had we just marched into a rhino's path? The consequence of that could be fatal, as rhinos have a fearsome reputation.

They have very poor eyesight but they make up for it with their sense of smell. If this rhino was close by, maybe hidden behind scrub or trees, it would smell us before we saw it, so it could soon be barrelling towards us with great speed and surprising agility.

We inspected the fresh footprints further and, by the spray of dirt and a few bird prints over the top of them, we judged they were from this morning. Still, we were annoyed at ourselves for having let our guards down. We continued on after the blood trail, while keeping a very keen eye on our surroundings.

We'd only travelled another hundred metres or so before my eyes flew open wide at the sight of the impala lying camouflaged by a circle of scrub, where it had fallen down, dead. I dragged it out of the scrub and into a clear patch of dirt. Finally, Amber and I could celebrate! Our grins went from ear to ear as we high-fived each other while yahooing at our accomplishment. This was a good sized buck.

We quickly sobered as we realised how late in the afternoon it was. We now had the task of breaking down the meat in an hour or so, as we would then need to be shut in our boma by dusk. This would be a hard task if we were at full strength, but in our weakened state I hoped it was not going to be impossible.

Leaving the animal until the next day wasn't an option as it was unlikely to last the night with all the scavengers in the area. Leaving out a fresh kill would also attract predators like lions and hyenas, which was the last thing we needed. I thought for a moment about the potential impact of us having fresh meat in our boma.

We went straight into gutting it where we were, so the blood and guts were disposed of well away from our camp. My machete was blunter than a butter knife and would not slice the hide open, so I had to resort to using the broad head of our arrow.

With Amber's help, I made the carcass into a backpack in our usual Kiwi style, so I could carry the meat back to camp. After I'd made a few slices with the blade of the arrow, I was able to loop the front legs through the rear legs, making two shoulder straps. I brushed aside the thought that I might be in too weak a state to carry the impala back even though it was heavier than me, perhaps 70 kilograms or more, and we were on our eighth day with no food.

I knelt down while Amber shuffled the carcass onto my back as I threaded my arms through the shoulder straps. This was the moment of truth. Were my legs going to hold up under its weight? We had both worked up a sweat from the rushed task under the strain of the lowering sun. There was no way we could let this meat not make it back to camp.

I could feel my determination running hot through my veins as, with a heave, Amber helped me to me feet. I took off back to camp with a strength I didn't know I had left in me. My extreme weakness and fatigue faded for a bit, and I took full advantage of this new strength. I didn't dare stop until we reached camp.

There was a tree right next to our boma that had a shoulder height 'V' in it, made by two branches. Amber and I slid the carcass off my back, hooking its horns into the 'V' in the tree.

Now it was hanging, it would be much easier to skin and we could keep the meat clean.

We both went flat stick into skinning it and made a conscious effort not to put holes in the hide as we wanted to cure it to use for shoes. With a blunt machete and small broad-head arrow tip to do the job, it was much harder than it needed to be, but Amber and I could see the escaping sun meant we only had minutes left before we needed to be back in the safety of our boma. Once it was skinned, we cut off the back straps and eye fillets. These are the best cuts of meat, so we would feast on them that night. The eye fillets and back straps were four decent cuts of meat, so they would provide us with four days' worth of meals.

The whole impala had a lot of meat on it, which could feed us until the end of the challenge if we could find some way of preserving it then rationed it hard. We didn't have time to break it down fully, but we had separated most of it from the carcass. We hastily carried the remains of the carcass away from camp, so it would not draw in any predators.

With the last of our strength, we threw each leg of meat, the head and the bundled skin up to the top of the spiky trees around our camp. We dragged up all the spiky branches from our barrier at the water hole and repurposed them by jamming them into the bottom of the trees we'd thrown the meat into. We hoped this would make it impossible for any animal to climb the trees to get to the meat. We thought about keeping the meat in our boma, so we could be sure it would be protected, but having a huge amount of raw meat in with us risked attracting leopards and lions.

Amber and I grinned at each other, satisfied that the thorny branches would protect our meat. In the last remaining minutes before dusk, we rushed down to the water hole to wash all the blood off us – we didn't want to be bait for predators that night! We then pulled our spiky door into our boma entrance behind us and readied ourselves for one hell of a night.

We had both searched the boma for the perfect stick with a forked end on it to cook our meat on. Then we sliced 5-centimetre squares of thick, juicy, red meat, off the eye fillet cut, and began cooking it. The edges crisped over the fire adding some charcoal flavouring. Our mouths salivated as we watched it cook. The first mouthful of succulent meat was indescribably scrumptious. We ate slowly, savouring each mouthful as we went.

We feasted until our bellies tightened with the strain of the food. We were wrong in thinking our stomachs would only be able to handle a small amount, having had no food for days. We treated ourselves with at least the equivalent of a dinner plate of meat that night, knowing we would be strictly rationing it in the days to come.

With the darkness came the cackling of hyenas and the terrifying roar of lions. We sharpened the spears we had made and lined up a few branches ready to burn the ends for torches to wave around. We spent the whole night shouting into the darkness as the animal noises closed in. We were unable to see anything, but we could hear an abundance of animal activity.

In the silence of the early hours of the morning, nearing 3 am, I'd only been dozing for a few minutes when I woke to the sound of panting right next to my ear! A hyena was right there, only metres away, with just our boma keeping us from being savaged.

Still in a dozing state, I leapt to my feet and yelled aggressively as I grabbed a burning branch from the fire, spraying hot embers across the ground as I went. I heard it back off into the darkness as Amber got to her feet.

In the little bit of light thrown out by my burning branch, Amber saw the faint outline of a leopard. With wide, alarmed eyes, she grabbed the machete and bashed it on the pot, making a deafening noise. She grabbed another burning branch to add to the chaos. This charade carried on for the entire night and we were glad to see the light coming up in the early hours of the morning, bringing with it the promise of soon being able to rest.

While we wanted to rest, we couldn't. We were too eager to see how much of our meat was still hanging in the trees, if any at all. From all the activity in the night, we already felt despair as we guessed not much meat would be left. We had plans to turn the meat into the traditional South African biltong, or jerky as we know it. This could preserve our meat so it would last a long time without rotting.

On inspection, we found that our meat in the top of the trees was still there, all intact and untouched. Amber and I both beamed and cheered in celebration. Our plan had worked *and* we had survived the night with a bunch of meat hanging around us. Today, we were going to break down all the meat and preserve it. We couldn't have another sleepless night with all this meat hanging around.

Our morale was sky high, but our strength had not returned. Amber and I still felt extremely weak and fatigued and were now beginning to understand the full impact of the salt-flavoured water we'd been living off. We thought the salty water was only making us feel extremely thirsty, and that it was the zero food that left us with no strength. But with full bellies, we knew the water was playing a big part in it. We were just under half-way through our challenge, so we hoped we could hold on while we looked for a new water source.

We grabbed the legs of meat down from the trees, then heaved them into our boma where we could cut them up next to the warmth of our fire. It was a nice change not having to spend the day shivering in the shade of our blind.

We sliced up all four legs, roughly 40 kilograms of meat, into thin slices. The thinner the better, but our machete and arrow heads were blunt, so this wasn't straight forward. We managed to get them down to roughly a centimetre thick, which wasn't ideal, but it would do.

In a tree that was nice and close to our boma, we hung the hundreds of pieces of meat to dry, secured by the spikes on each branch. If we had done this in New Zealand's humid air, the meat would have rotted, but we were in the dry season in South Africa, and the meat dried better than we could have hoped. Some of it was completely dry by the end of the first day so we took these pieces down to store. These mouthfuls of meat would have to be strictly rationed. Even with all of this dried meat, we would still only have a couple of mouthfuls each for our remaining days out here. We were confident we could survive on this even if we didn't hunt anymore, so our priority shifted to finding a new water source.

The following day, our task was to use the brains to tan the impala hide so we could make shoes out of it. It was a massive effort to flesh the hide in our fatigued state. Once it was done, we found a ring of small trees where we stretched out the hide to dry.

I smashed open the impala's skull, which we had set aside, and removed the brain. I mixed this with warm water until it had a milkshake consistency and then spread the mixture on the hide to tan it. A brain milkshake makes an emulsifying solution, which helps to break down the membrane on the hide, so it's soft enough to make clothing or shoes.

Without being able to wait any longer, and with our impala-hide shoes on our feet, we then set out in search of a better water source.

THE IMPORTANCE OF ATTITUDE

Attitude is everything in tough situations and it is amazing how something as small as a positive attitude can make all the difference. A good attitude seems to pull you through anything and make everything OK, no matter how bad or tough the situation might be. There is good in every situation and that's the part, as big or as little as it may be, to try to focus on when things are tough.

Even if you don't realise it at the time, negativity brings down the atmosphere. It can bring down your frame of mind, your morale and your will. Everything feels better and seems possible when you have a positive attitude. After all, the world is neither against you nor for you. The reality is that you create your own narrative – so why not create one where the world is *for* you?

In challenges, a good attitude can be as important as skill or ability, yet the role it plays is often skipped over. If your attitude going into a challenge is, 'It's too hard' or 'I can't manage that', then this is likely what your result will be, as you have set yourself up not to achieve. You have programmed the direction your challenge is likely to take.

Instead, go into a challenge with a good attitude. Believe that you can conquer it and, if you don't complete your challenge, then at least you'll know you've given it a bloody good go, which is what it is all about!

We like to look each and every challenge in the eye, give it a menacing grin and say, 'Challenge accepted!'

OUT OF THE WILDERNESS

Chapter 14

Out of the Wilderness

South Africa

SERENA

We'd been surviving on a few mouthfuls a day of our rationed impala biltong, and it was still a tasty treat to look forward to each day. Surprisingly, we felt quite content with these rations. But now that the end was near, we had begun indulging in discussions of food, glorious foooood! We could hardly contain ourselves as we talked through what our first meal was going to be and discussed all the sugary delights we would be inhaling once we got back to civilisation.

At around the Day 10 mark, we'd both been craving big, carby meals. They weren't strong cravings, just enough that the thought would pop into our heads. At that point, we never dwelt on the cravings, but they became a fun topic to occupy us. We spent hours talking through what food we could go for about now, and we'd discuss the fine, intricate details of each new meal we could think of: a thick bread sandwich with peanut butter, cucumber and tasty cheese; a hearty plate of spaghetti bolognaise; creamy bacon and egg pasta; a banana with peanut butter spread on it; or a burger and hot chips. And so it went on as we revisited each option numerous times.

Towards the end of the challenge, our cravings shifted as, unknown to us, our bodies needed sugar. The banana and peanut butter snack we'd craved on Day 10 had now turned into a banana with Nutella spread on it. We talked about the tubs of Nutella we were craving and the M&Ms we imagined pouring into the Nutella, then we'd discuss the Milky Bars or Kit Kats we'd dip into ice cream. (We'd never actually had these combinations before and they certainly weren't normal treats for us.)

A hot topic was all the different types of lollies, chocolate and homemade baking we would eat once we returned to New Zealand. Amber and I usually eat relatively healthily – although I will admit to having a bit of a sweet tooth – but craving all that sugar at once was very abnormal for us.

After crossing many miles in search of a better water source, we came across two brothers, Warren and Thomas, who were also doing the 21-day survival challenge for the show. We teamed up with them for the few remaining days. They were from Louisiana in the United States and we got on well with them. We all had similar skills and capabilities, so we were happy to combine them.

We had found a larger water hole, the colour of which was even worse than the small one Amber and I had left behind. It was green and soupy looking, and we dreaded the first taste, as we didn't know if we could handle more salty water.

I took one for the team and hesitantly sipped a mouthful from our pot once it had boiled and cooled. The floating chunks of unidentifiable matter were hard to swallow but, compared to the salty water we had been drinking, this tasted like it had come from a crystal clear spring. To quench our thirst, we practically sculled the murky yet delightful liquid.

We worked well with the brothers and were stoked to be teamed up with like-minded people. Having new people to yarn with was great for our sanity, as Amber and I had exhausted all possible conversation topics 10 times over.

It was Day 20 of our 21-day survival challenge in the South African wilderness and the end was so near we could almost taste it. We sat around our fire, happy in the knowledge that this time tomorrow, we would be gorging on copious amounts of food – if we could make it through the night and avoid falling prey to a leopard or lion on the trek out to our extraction point.

Despite our feeble states, we knew it was of the utmost importance that we remained alert and vigilant until we were physically out of the wilderness. Looking at our basic map, we could see the distance that we would have to cover to make it out of here and we knew it would take us many hours. Ideally, we would leave at the crack of dawn, so there would be no risk of getting caught out by the end of the day, resulting in an extra night in the wilderness.

Despite our eagerness, we still needed to steady ourselves. We could not switch off, as wild animals were still a constant and very real threat. We would have to wait until the sun was well up in the morning before we could leave the safety of our boma and embark on the journey out.

Amber and I were both in a weak, lethargic state and usually effortless tasks like walking exhausted our energy levels. Even so, we always seemed to be able to keep going when we needed to. It's amazing what the human body is capable of when pushed to its limits.

The salty water we'd been drinking and the lack of food had really taken a toll on our bodies. I thought I must have looked extremely malnourished but I only had to look at Amber as an indication of how I might be looking. She was certainly thinner than she had been 20 days ago and her long hair was thick with dust and leaves. Her face was crusted with dry dirt and ash from the fire, and her eyes were a little sunken, but overall, she didn't look half as bad as I felt. It was only her eyes that gave away that she was in the same weak state as I was.

Our skin was dry and cracked and our hips and shoulders were grazed raw from tossing and turning on the rough ground when we slept. We were covered in scratches, and my skin was super sensitive with a horrendous heat rash caused by the amount of time I'd spent practically sitting on the fire. Our hands were terribly weathered, and our fingernails were black from grime and the split skin was painfully receding around them.

The walk out was going to be strenuous, and we knew we would need to muster everything in our power, no matter how tough it was, to make it out of here. I hoped this was going to be enough, as there was no way we could make it this far and not make Day 21!

Although it felt as though our bodies were battling hard, the truth is the mental battle was just as tough, if not tougher. We'd spent most of our days hunting, which meant staying very still in our blind. While we were there, we talked about every topic we could possibly think of – multiple times. With our bodies deteriorating, fighting the cold and suffering from sleep deprivation, it became increasingly difficult to do things to occupy our minds. We are usually always on the go, doing several things at once, so slowing down to doing nothing for days on end was as harsh on our minds as the challenge had been on our bodies.

The ruthless winter nights never let up. This new location had been noticeably colder than our last camp. Amber and I tried everything to keep warm. We tried lighting multiple fires on either side of us, lying back-to-back for body warmth while having three fires surrounding us and burying a large pile of hot coals to lie on top of. We even accidentally lit our shelter on fire when we brought the fire in too close. Our roof caught alight and we leapt out hastily whacking it out with branches. After all our trial and error, we found the solution was to create a low, dome-shaped shelter and to pack the roof and walls very tightly with brush and foliage. The roof was only about mid-thigh high, which helped channel the warmth of the fire to where we lay.

Along with the prevalent hyenas, just three nights earlier we had had a very close call with a couple of sizable rhinos.

Now that our final night was here, the atmosphere was slightly different. The air was crackling with our excitement, and we were restless, unable to sit still. It was our last night before we would be able to have a shower, sit on something soft, lather our skin in much-needed moisturiser and eat, eat and eat. Our last evening drifted by and included a semi-peaceful dusk visit from a herd of elephants passing by. Nothing like the visit we had had from the lone bull elephant at our last camp.

Our excitement was coupled with a little sadness as we would be leaving the place that had been our home for the past three weeks. It was a beautiful place and we had had some magical moments here. You absolutely could not beat the late afternoons when we would sit on the sunny bank by our large water hole at this second camp. There, we were half camouflaged by some trees on the water's edge and we'd watch in disbelief as animals of all kinds came in for a drink. We'd watch great elephants, impalas, kudus, zebras and baboons and think about how breathtaking the undisturbed African wilderness is and how amazing it was that we were able to witness it.

By the early hours of the morning, we realised that trying to sleep was pointless so we sat up chatting excitedly in the darkness. When the sun finally peeped over the horizon, Day 21 had arrived, and the thrill of our journey out was buzzing in the air. As soon as it was light enough for us to leave the boma, we went to retrieve a pot of water to boil for the march ahead. We didn't know how long the extraction march was going to take and, already dehydrated, we knew it was too risky to try to speed things up by carrying less water.

Once the water had boiled, we scattered dirt over our low, smouldering, morning fire to put it out completely, and we laughed at the pitiful pile of belongings we'd gathered up. It consisted of our pot of water, machete, the bow and arrows and my impala skull, which I was determined to take with me.

Starting out, we moved quickly in the still brisk morning air, only stopping to pull thorns from our feet. Just over an hour in, that eagerness wore off as the heat of the mid-morning sun brought sweat to our foreheads. With every step, my feet felt like they were encased in buckets of cement. On top of this, Amber was unwell with a sore stomach, which meant our morale dropped a little.

Each time we rested in the shade, we reminded ourselves that we were so close to the luxuries of food, clean water and comfort, we just had to keep pushing. I did my best to spur Amber on. We focused on just taking one step after another in the hope that the end was close. But the end was not close.

We carried on for hours and hours as the sun angled its way past midday and into the afternoon. Soon I began to wonder if we'd gone off course, so when we next stopped to rest, we used our map and some landmarks to orientate ourselves before carrying on.

Despite our fatigue, we were on guard the entire time. We paused whenever we heard movement or thought we heard a grunt or growl. When that happened, we'd make lots of noise and throw rocks, then we'd only move on when we were sure any potential threats were no longer there. At one point, Amber came dangerously close to stepping on a venomous snake – the first one we'd seen this whole time, as they hibernate in winter.

As we arrived at a clearing, we both thought we'd heard a vehicle. Trying to decide if it was too good to be true, we froze in our tracks, listening to confirm our suspicions that the low rumble we'd heard was actually a vehicle.

Moments later, a vehicle popped out of the scrub into the clearing. All of a sudden, all my fighting efforts melted into a graceful, joyous rush towards the vehicle and we started cheering uncontrollably. We couldn't believe it – we'd made it!

Getting to the end of such a tough challenge felt amazing. After all the trials and tribulations, the highs and lows, we were finally here at the end. I felt on top of the world. We had set out to see if we could survive in the wilderness for 21 days, we had tested ourselves mentally and physically and we had done it!

Now that the challenge was over, the film crew and producers were finally able to interact with us. We all cheered and hooted as they joined in the celebrations – they were as happy as we were. We'd done it – we'd really done it!

All the celebrations and thanking everyone well and truly exhausted the last tiny little bits of energy we had left, but smiles still beamed across our faces. The crew got out dressing gowns and a little cooler bag for each of us. It almost felt as though the dressing gowns were not necessary, and I thought about how strange it was that being naked felt so normal and I was totally comfortable in my own skin. Despite this, I gladly put on my dressing gown and the soft fabric against my skin felt magical. Before the challenge, I never noticed how soft this same dressing gown had felt. It was now a luxury, and I felt like the luckiest person in the world to have it.

We looked into our cooler bags and our eyes nearly popped out of our heads and our grins could not have been bigger. We couldn't believe the crew had actually gone to the effort of grabbing all the treats we'd been dreaming up. We were miked the whole time, so they'd heard every word we'd said – and we must have gone over it hundreds of times! Even so, they must have travelled for hours to get to a village that sold all these sweets.

We wasted no time looking. We dived straight into our goodie bags and ripped open the Nutella, the M&Ms and the Milky Bars. We spread peanut butter on our bananas and we cracked open our cans of Sprite and Coke.

Even though we were as eager as children waking up on Christmas morning, we ate slowly and with purpose, savouring all the flavours that were exploding in our mouths. Interestingly, in just those few minutes of eating sugar, my teeth became furry and I felt like I needed to brush them. During the entire challenge my teeth had felt clean and fresh, even though I'd only had a stick I'd chewed into bristles to brush them.

After a few hours on the back of the extraction vehicle, we arrived at the small village where we would stay in a hotel for the night. They had a table set, ready for us. Again, we couldn't believe that everything we'd talked about was there waiting for us.

We were still in an extremely remote area and the village only had this one hotel, so we were in absolute disbelief that they could fulfil our requests. In our dressing gowns, still filthy, we sat down to eat. We had burgers, fries, pizza, sandwiches, ice cream, cake – we ate until our hearts were content. Our usual diet consists of a lot of vegetables, but we didn't crave them at all – we just felt like sugar and burgers!

Once we had feasted like animals and eaten three days' worth of food in one sitting, we had another new experience to look forward to – having a shower and washing our hair!

Amber and I got to our room, and I lay down on my bed and couldn't believe how luxurious having a mattress felt. This was something I'd previously taken for granted and it now felt like the most unbelievable experience. The softness absorbed my body and lying down didn't make me ache.

Simultaneously, we rushed to contact our partners and family. We hadn't missed our phones one single bit and almost didn't want to turn them on, but we were bursting to tell our loved ones we were still alive and that we had survived this gruelling challenge.

Of course, there was no way to settle who got the first shower other than the trusty, dusty paper, scissors, rock. I yelled and hooted as I was first to win three rounds, and I raced to the shower. I washed my hair about five times to get out all the dirt while Amber waited impatiently.

When I stepped out of the shower all clean, I felt like a new person. Then I moisturised my skin to the hills and back.

After a night in the hotel, it was time to embark on our 36-hour trip home. This consisted of several plane rides, during which we pretty much ate the whole time. Even though we were full to the very brim with food, and we both felt uncomfortably bloated, we couldn't help it. We just kept eating every time we were near food.

We were fully aware that our bodies were in starvation mode, which was why we wanted to carry on eating, but we didn't care and gave into the cravings anyway. It got so bad that we both had painful stomachs that were beyond bloated, yet our subconsciouses still said, 'More food!'

It was even hard to walk through the airport to catch our flight, yet we still carried on eating whenever we could.

When we got home, I felt like I had a new outlook on life and I was seeing everything for the first time. A lot of little things I'd never thought about before, and had very much taken for granted, were now the big things in life. The luxury of sitting on a chair, or a soft, cushy couch, the protection that clothes and shoes give, being warm, taking a hot bath or shower, sleeping in a soft, warm bed, having a pantry full of food – the list goes on. It now seemed an exciting concept that we could simply go to the supermarket and buy any food we wanted.

It took our skin many weeks of moisturising to fully heal and get back to how it used to be. Our bruised hips took weeks to return to normal. Our shoulders, which felt as if they would dislocate when we lay on our sides, took more than three months to heal. I was astonished to find we'd lost 6–8 kilograms each on the challenge, but I had easily put on 10 kilograms within a few weeks of being back home, as I did a lot of overeating.

Before the challenge, I'd been so hectic with work, rushing through life, always on the run. Having my own business consumed a large portion of my time and, although I squeezed in adventures around it, I had not had time to do a lot of the little things I'd wanted to do. I hadn't spent the time I would have liked with my partner, family and friends.

The challenge had given me a real wake-up call, to recalibrate back to a balanced lifestyle. I am thankful this adventure enabled me to reflect on my life, on what is really important to me. The bonds and friendships we have with family and friends bring us so much joy and they are the ones who can help us get through anything. Sometimes, spending time with family and friends can be the first thing we sacrifice when life gets busy, but with constant reflection we can always reprioritise, to put the important things first.

BELIEVE IN YOURSELF

SERENA

During my time in the South African wilderness, I learnt many lessons, but one saying that resonates with me is, 'Whether you think you can or you think you can't – you're usually right!' Our beliefs and mindsets are very powerful tools and having them on your side will put you ahead in any challenge you take on.

Your mindset can determine your level of success, so believing in yourself is crucial. Your mind can be your strongest ally as well as your worst enemy. It can be the thing that pushes you through your toughest challenges and it can be the thing that stops you in your tracks.

If you are taking on a challenge or striving for a goal and it seems too big, it can help to break it down into small steps until you reach a point where you believe you can do it. You can grow your self-belief from there.

Backing yourself is something that has to come from within. It helps when others are supportive and believe in you, but the most important thing is the belief that comes from within, which in turn gives others the confidence to believe in you as well. This self-assurance is what keeps you moving forward when you are faced with difficulties.

Having a positive outlook and believing in yourself is something that can be trained, just like any physical muscle in the body. Some people naturally have this positive energy, while some of us need to work hard to squash any negativity and self-doubt and to build up self-belief in its place. Either way, the more time and effort we put into ourselves, the more that self-belief will come naturally.

Mindset is something Amber and I have had to constantly focus on through many of our challenges. We have found that, during adventures like climbing a mountain or surviving in the wilderness, it is the mind and self-belief that pushes the body, so sometimes strength of mind is even more important than physical strength. Believe in yourself and your achievements will follow.

EPILOGUE

Epilogue

*Get the most out of life
and enjoy the journey*

AMBER AND SERENA

Sometimes, it's easy to get sucked into the hustle and bustle of life, which can stop us from doing the things we enjoy. We all have reasons (also known as excuses) why we aren't doing the things we want to be doing, but when we are able toas beingpush past our excuses to do the things we love to do, we get so much more out of life.

Take a moment now to think ajourney. The things you really want to do and the way you want to live your life. When you look back on your life (no matter how many years young you are), what are the key moments that stick out to you? In your fondest memories, what were you doing? Do you remember those weekends you stayed home or said no to an opportunity? Or do you remember that weekend when you went on an epic hike? Or the weekend you caught up with your friends and had a laugh? Or the weekend you took that awesome camping trip with the kids? Whatever it is for you, whatever those fond memories are, that's what you need to do more of, and that's where your joy comes from.

The reality is — and this is a quote we think true — 'If it's important, you will find a way. If it's not important, you will find an excuse.' Sometimes, when we have excuses we believe are unavoidable, we simply need a wake-up call to prioritise what's most important to us.

After reading some of our adventures you may be asking why we take on these challenges. It may seem like we've faced a lot of hardship, and you may be wondering if it was enjoyable. The answer is yes, it certainly was! And we wouldn't trade these adventures for anything.

We don't look at the hard parts of adventures as being unenjoyable, and these hurdles should not be seen as negative, as they are far from it. All adventures and challenges have hard parts to them. It is these that test how badly we want something. After all, if every challenge were easy, would it be much of a challenge?

We accept these hard parts as part of the journey and continue on. Often, the more demanding the task we are faced with, the greater the accomplishment we feel once we've completed it.

Whether we're experiencing the good or bad parts, the journey is what keeps the fire of life alive. Each little win along the way to reaching your goal should be celebrated.

I believe having goals is very important, but sometimes we can be so focused on the final destination that we forget to enjoy the journey. Focusing only on the end point can be detrimental to motivation, especially if it is taking longer than you anticipated to get there.

We need to make time to enjoy the littlealso keepings along the way. The wins, the losses, the highs and the lows are all part of a fulfilling journey. The trials and tribulations you face may seem as though it's not working out, but it's a funny old world — at a certain point, you will look back and see how everything was actually falling into place, although you couldn't see it at the time.

In all the things we do, life is what you make it. We are all dealt a different hand, and it's how you choose to react to that hand that will determine the way that experience goes. Just enjoy the journey and the destination will come.

Acknowledgements

We would like to thank our mother and father for raising us right, for always encouraging us to get out there while also keeping us grounded at the same time, for leading by example, for inspiring us, for teaching us that anything is possible, and for being all-round goers!

We would also like to thank our partners for their continued support and encouragement, and our two sisters, who inspire in their own ways.